THE CIRCULAR INCANTATION

ESSENTIAL POETS SERIES 206

Canada Council for the Arts / Conseil des Arts du Canada

ONTARIO ARTS COUNCIL / CONSEIL DES ARTS DE L'ONTARIO

50 YEARS OF ONTARIO GOVERNMENT SUPPORT OF THE ARTS
50 ANS DE SOUTIEN DU GOUVERNEMENT DE L'ONTARIO AUX ARTS

Guernica Editions Inc. acknowledges the support of the Canada Council for the Arts and the Ontario Arts Council. The Ontario Arts Council is an agency of the Government of Ontario. We acknowledge the financial support of the Government of Canada through the Canada Book Fund (CBF) for our publishing activities.

THE CIRCULAR INCANTATION

An Exercise In Loss And Findings

Irene Marques

GUERNICA
TORONTO – BUFFALO – LANCASTER (U.K.) 2013

Michael Mirolla, editor
Guernica Editions Inc.
P.O. Box 76080, Abbey Market, Oakville,
(ON), Canada L6M 3H5
2250 Military Road, Tonawanda, N.Y. 14150-6000 U.S.A.

Distributors:
University of Toronto Press Distribution,
5201 Dufferin Street, Toronto (ON), Canada M3H 5T8
Gazelle Book Services, White Cross Mills,
High Town, Lancaster LA1 4XS U.K.

Book design by Jamie Kerry of Belle Étoile Studios
www.belleetoilestudios.com

First edition.
Printed in Canada.

Legal Deposit – Third Quarter

Library of Congress Catalog Card Number: 2013933974

Library and Archives Canada Cataloguing in Publication

Marques, Irene, 1969-
The circular incantation : an exercise in loss and findings / Irene Marques.
(Essential poets series ; 206) Poems.
Also issued in electronic format.
ISBN 978-1-55071-735-8
I. Title. II. Series: Essential poets series ; 206
PS8626.A683C57 2013 C811'.6 C2013-901451-9

To Grandmother Beatriz
To Father Adelino
To Mother Alzira
To Isabel

And as always, to the Goats of Adsamo

Contents

The making of love 11
I am unravelling 12
Taking photographs 13
The first knight 17
There are flowers growing out of me 18
Dressing me up 21
The beautiful face of sadness 23
The kissing of the floor 27
Magnificent shadows 29
Dreaming of crosses 32
In the moment 33
The idea 34
The pulsating of my temporal lobe 36
The event of my becoming 37
Friday 39
Friday still 41
I have come from far away 43
The traveller 44
My garden and yours 45
The circularity of hydrangeas or the garden of O 46
Release 47
The top of my foot. 49
My body is full of water. 51

I live on top of the world 53
The mountain dweller. 55
The house without mirrors. 56
I live. 58
Living still 61
Living again 64
The feeling of the frog. 68
Black magnolias 70
Imagining sorrow 72
The middle of the road 74
The miracle of the round pot. 77
The perception of colours. 78
Praying the rosary 80
The mountain pianist 82
The morning dew 84
The story of the old woman 87
The human settlement 90
Healing again, Or the dream of South Africa 92
The station of the central 95
The intimacy of love. 98
The sonnet of red roses 102
I will see you in the winter 104
The last supper (or the first) 106
The making of beautiful stories 108
The making of sense. 110
Modes of reading 112
Maydays of my youth 114

The time of cherries 116
Earthing my body 118
If you 120
I wait for you. 121
I wait for you again 123
I wait for you again and again 124
Craving for you 127
Isabel, In the death of my body 130
My body becoming 133
Coming upon you 134
Bleeding for the being. 135
My body comes 137
Coming from deep 138
I look for you. 140
I am a novel, A novel of my own making 146

ABOUT THE AUTHOR. 149

ABOUT HER WORK. 150

The only words that deserve
to exist are words
that are better than silence.

– Juan Carlos Onetti

The making of love

I make love to you when you are asleep. Between the fog of my mind and the rain of your body we join, down by the luminous lake-river channel. There are caves of concaves, millions of them, tumultuous and sliding curves enlacing the being that we are. My arms open up the wideness, and we, the being becoming, become joined by the navel. The navel takes us away to the source to the eucalyptus tree planted in the incantatory garden by our ancestral father. In the big plaza. When one molecule said yes to another and love was made for the first time. In the world where we lived before dancing in this platform. I slide down, down onto you, and the flora of our being, which is the flora of the world, awakens us. We become incandescent smelling roses and geraniums, edelweisses and hydrangeas. I am a lily you are a rose. The making, marking of love.

I am unravelling

I am unravelling like a novel of my own making, my mother told me to write lighter stuff otherwise I would become crazy, crazy as they come, crazy like my older sister Otília. I am unravelling like a novel of my own making. I am running you now. I have been running from you all my life, feeding you with merely tangible lines so that you don't fall into the dark well where she has gone. My sister. Like my mother says, she has gone down, down there, to the well of the river-lake where the caves full of concaves sink you into loneliness and fantastic shadows. Shadows that take the blood from her veins and the moist from her speaking tongue. She forgets how to kiss, how to open the arm wide, my mother … I am unravelling like a novel of my own. My mother will forget, forgive my imperfection, and that of my sister.

Taking photographs

I take shots of crickets that live in their holes, of the grasshoppers that stutter trying to fly great distances in windy days

I take shots of the spaces between my fingers and the back of my bone – trying to find the memory of my pain because if I see it I can then paint upon it – imprint roses and breeding bread, roses and slow incantations and then I will make anew what I always knew I could and would be after some concentrated exercise, the type that requires shallow breathing and stillness of the body – the final touch-up of the great media artist – fading away the bleeding bubbling particles that damage the perfect

I take shots of my back inverting my body to immeasurable somersaults and then I see the ribs that make me and align my shadow with the altitude of life

I take the camera even further down, down of myself and I enter the moist moss down below – becoming acquainted with Pluto – I converse with him because he is in a good mood, optimistic of the moment – he guides me through the tortuous channels that life is before becoming life in the pulsating of the upstairs window

I allow him to give me his hand, moistened from the dew down there, because at first I am afraid of losing who I am in the muddy humid overland of the below – and then, after his patience teaches me the way, I walk freely and motivated, alone, unafraid to remember where I come from and where I will return, after I live the life I am when I am not filming this film taking this photograph

I swim with such dexterity now that all the underworld seems to be a very familiar site – an intimate one even, as if my blood remembers the humidity that I have always been by the power of some incantation that stayed alive in the surface of my skin, crawling upon me like a quilt of the transcendent – travelling certain and concrete to the river vessels of my brain – the lymph nodes that keep me alert to the trans-nationality of my being, the splendorous Hollywood of my long time career

I emerge from there returning to the upper levels of existence and then I take more shots to add to my already complex long line of *películas*

I take shots of the dark spaces of the moon, of the shadows of the white roses and the underlying movements of the light blue hydrangeas, of the bridges underneath the rail train capturing the noises of the screeching wheels when they pass above me, or the perfect moving silence that appears in the eyes of the passengers of life who sit there unaware of their awareness, being conducted by the great conductor of this line

I also take presence of the saints at the church – of Saint Laura and Saint Amelia who lie side by side in their perfect eternal poses, decorations to the altar – Madonnas of all time, I touch their faces and see the effigies that they have become to preserve beauty and the virginity of being – the Buddhas of the orient in the adoration that is required by thee

I film the Day of All Saints – by a miracle of unseen force my camera imprints the impressions of the many that have moved to the crust below where I have just been, as photographed above – their transparent presences transpire through the magnetic field that is my camera, a somersault to the visible invisible

I cross the altar slowly, like a butterfly priest incanting the eternal mass evoked and invoked over and over through the vast lazy centuries, and I take shots of me, of you, of the baptisms that have been performed since Christianity became a religion to be followed by believers, of the brides who have swept that cold clear floor that is the altar with their long beautiful white dresses trying to rescue the mime of the true truth, like innocent children born to execute the marvellous and make things forever lasting

I shoot the arias and the nuptial marches and that secret moment when the body and the blood of Christ enter my mouth and yours making us cannibals of the divine

I then shoot the voice of the priest of the last rites performing the *última missa* for my darling friend Isabel who died last fall in that sullen November – I capture his breath as he incants the words that will allow her to escape the devil's paws and enter the golden gate of heaven or the garden, the garden of O – I approach the casket and I see her, Isabel, in a white dress, dressed for the gods, I dreamed of her like that, *noiva em branco para Deus*, even he needs a virgin to feast upon, I dreamed of her like that the night before she died – I see roses and roses upon her frail body eaten by the leech of cancer – I see roses and roses upon her frail body incanting it before it forever goes – cell by cell – bone by bone – even the marrow – that sacred humidity of life where everything lies

I go deeper inwards and I photograph her entrails still intact, at least to the visible eye, and then I wait longer and

I see the primal worms at work attacking her core, and then I stay there staring in concentration with my lens and I see her form going and going, disintegrating the inner walls and bursting into the white satin and fleecy clouds of the house she was put in after her heart said: "No, no more, no more, because death is my final destination, my ultimate *abraço!*" – and then ahead, much ahead, my lens captures the other forms, the ones that she will become because becoming is her fortune and mine too – as a final act of this film my camera sinks down below again and SHE becomes spattered, in the walls – portrait of the unswayable – my beloved friend Isabel

I still shoot the word INRI on the cross holding that famous man who died for all of us of this religion – I fix my lens attentively on it staying there for longer than I remember how to tell you and then the world under inspection transmutes to a long vast poem that I cannot contain in me, for it evades the small iris of my filming vision – but then I move slightly so that I can get the perfect angle and my vision field becomes all the poetry that is possible to shoot under the canvas of being

I take shots and shots because my world and yours is everywhere I turn
I am a camera all over my body, filming me, filming you and all the spaces that lay between us

The first knight

The first knight comes to me when I am in the depths of loss, in the eternal sleep or the dark togetherness

When I sit unaware in the realm of unconditional love, when I have forgiven, forgotten myself – and dwell only in that imperceptible crevice that allows my eye to fix memory in the perfect spot for many instants, enough to recall that which had evaded the concave shell that my body is, a body whose pulse and noise exist in themselves, and yet they often slip through my being, unnoticed by the strong current of the other logics that also mark, make my presence

The first knight comes to me like that, in unexpected moments, when I first doubt the possibility of life, and then as an unpredictable chain of fierce events, I awake to the biggest sense of grounding, a compact sediment at the bottom of myself, a river with a heavy bed, reminding me of the astonishing weight and presence that my sole being, my sole logic are, arousing me to the wonders of the knight that brought me to me, and I am mediated through the current and heavy chain of his thick, thick hug preceded by nothing – the unprecedented event

The first knight comes to me when I am in the vacant of the vacancy, in holidays for eternal nameless moments, in places untraceable, untraced by the letters of my rosary or the gargling of my visceral purple liquid, when I am blind and blind and blind again

There are flowers growing out of me

There are flowers growing out of me
In the valley of my being I see roses after roses after roses
River of empty spaces where there is more than the fragrance of my being

I breathe slowly and peacefully
Like a baby just born
With that certitude of life that fools no one and needs no further explanation

I look above the valley that is my womb and the peak that is my head
And I see
I see roses and roses and roses
And I smile with the certainty of the fragrance dancing in the air that is the sky of my soul

I lay down and caress the earth, the pure soil of South Africa
Where blood has been spoiled for centuries for love of the land
That red land, with soft clay that you can manipulate to make alive the ancestors of your house
The dance, the carnival of life brought into extricate existence
By the old lords of civilization

There are men who have killed for that land and for the diamonds that lay beautiful underneath where they keep scintillating light into the crust above where we walk and lay and grow flowers

If only they were left there, where they belong
If only they had been left underneath, in the sacred
darkness that creates pure illumination

Then I would lay still for centuries to come, in pure
adoration towards the skies
Undulating my body in sensual movements
Praying to the Gods that had been at work all these millennia
Watching over the men and the greed that keeps corrupting
their being

If only they had been left underneath, I could stay here
with my body to the ground
Kneeling in a perpetual kiss, embroidering the fragrance
that emanates from the dark beautiful core of the land
where we live and walk and grow flowers

If only they had been left underneath, I would stay here in
eternal adoration of the skies
Without being afraid to soil my laying resting body in the
blood that has gone down in the name of thee – because
they say pearls are forever
I would stay here with my body to the ground
Kneeling in perpetual adoration
Praising the laws that make us all so human and
fundamentally beautiful

There are flowers growing out of me
In the valley of my being
Roses after roses after roses
And I get lost in the pure fragrance of my being
And I cry for those who now feed that body of mine, and
yours too if you pay proper attention to the slow movements
of your limbs when they are tired of the day's events

There are flowers growing out of me
And I get lost in the fragrance of my being
Laying there in pure contemplation and adoring the sun
above

There are flowers growing
Calling into you, whose soul might be wandering
In the azure that stares from that empty scintillating space
above and all around me
That abyss of the infinite light where we all are

There are flowers
Bleeding the life of those who have passed away in the
name of thee
Because pearls are eternal

Dressing me up

I ask you to dress me up from top to bottom
Start with the hair, put *missangas* on my braids, colourful and thick and noisy
The ones that come from Africa, use many, as many as you can so that my head becomes a full multicolour astounding abyss with the shadows of the stunning Dark Continent illuminating the rest of the planet

Put full coloured earrings on my ears, the organs that bring me sounds of the beautiful – choose those with the wideness of un-ending circles, of chanting wind, when I, like a woman of this world, run in slow motion throughout the sands of placid beaches and humid deserts – but adorn them only after you have crossed them slowly with your moist porous cells so that I can keep hearing music for the rest of my living life and then after when I cross the water bridge and enter the fluid realm of blind catharsis

Then move to the neck elegant and straight
Use colours from the Maasai queens – bright and red and incendiary green making me the rainbow that crosses between this planet and all the others

And slowly, like the dance of the white butterfly, come to my chest protruding with breathing force and erected with brown nipples that become reddish with desire when you paint them with the colour of your intimate tongue and the message of your white sharp teeth – a cannibal of the adorable

And then fly or swim to my belly – the womb of you and me and the little ones that will come after you finish dressing me up – crown it with silver pearls and white magnolias from the wide desert and myrrh and eucalyptus incense and branches of yellows, mimosas making me the spring ripe with precious metals and the plants of eternity there, dancing in me, making me the dancer of dancers, *a dançarina menina*

And then you must go further down, for it is even more sublime
When you enter the concave cave that lies there in the space that you need to fill, take all the necessary precautions not to disturb my mineral *império*
Carve narrow channels first with your small fingers where you will plant tiny little blue flowers and lilac too – the two that I prefer
Make circular rounds until the water amounts itself telling you that plants do indeed grow inside me

Make other rounds with all the possessions you have in your body and in the impeccable taste of your soul of ancient knight
And then do not stop there
Descend further down and plant carnations and red tulips in each of my legs
Silver roses in each of my feet
Small lilies in each of my toes
And finalize the feast with sprinkles of yellow mimosas (again) and also the little blue and lilac flowers – the ones that I prefer making me the quilt of this land – the impeccable road that you have walked upon with the care that you follow to become the prince that you are

Dress me up
Incanting my beautiful body with prophecies of the untold

The beautiful face of sadness

Clara Maria is a sad woman
She comes to you with flawless dark rings and motives implanted in her face
When you first see her you do not know how to speak to her, how to tell her of the promise that the daybreak may bring when the first glitter of fresh light filters through the window of your soul and you remember in awe, the awe of a pure child, how the witness of being can be so beautiful

When you first see her you do not know how to offer her your own sorrow because the story she brings to you, in the full extent of her life, is so much grander so much more important

You think of something, something that will erase, just a little bit, the lines that make her who she is – Clara Maria, Maria Clara – where is your clarity?

You walk timidly to her and try to show your extended hand in the direction of her being horizontally or vertically in an attempt to find the way

You slow down your own self, even obliterating your own breathing, so that she can feel that the world is all there at her knees wanting her to be happy and gay, walking steadily throughout the ways of the world, sure that there will be a way, even if at the very end, sure that love and forgiveness can be encountered

You dress in very neutral colours, almost invisible in fact, and try to make her see the astounding beauty of her own dress – Clara Maria, Maria Clara – where is your light?

You walk backwards to her in slow, slow incantation, as if you were praying and playing, praying and playing, pretending that you do not really see the immense sadness of her eyes, her cheeks, and the cells that in there do not live

You make a slow dance in circles of bright glitters that you stole from your own happy moments and you put it in her elbows as if that is the true place that will transmit the way to the rest of Clara Maria's being

You kneel down beside her, not in front of her because you know, in your true sensitivity, the sensitivity of someone who has been there, that open sorrow for the victimized other is not the proper medicine to bring about redemption and the straight way of life

You lay down on your belly and wipe her feet with a clean, white, all cotton handkerchief soaking all the dirt and all the blood that are intruding on its health and preventing Clara Maria from moving unburdened, without the freight of her moment – and then, after all the wiping, you kiss each feet and each toe, one and the other, one and two and three and four and five, one and two and three and four and five

You murmur something, which is not a song but which you think has the cadence of a slow, slow flute announcing itself in the middle of the beautiful undulating field of wheat

You become a tulip in disguise and a lily in slow opening mode trying to call to Maria Clara her own hidden power that might, must exist down there, in some area of her hollowness and very large way

You sublimate yourself and make love to the pollen that dances in front of you and you show her all the movements that you make with splendid accuracy, patient and sure that the stone must lay somewhere in Maria Clara's under-being and is only tardive in disclosing itself, perhaps afraid of the upper sides, or perhaps only because it needs to be taught how to swim in air and dance in sea

You send invisible breaths of incensed perfume gathered from the gardens of memorial bougainvilleas that you have kept in you since your visit to the many sunny places where they live

You come closer and closer to her face, and in a bold moment of fundamental fraternity, you hug her in close, close tightness, forgetting the boundaries of your own being and the weighty sadness of Maria Clara

You wait in pure expectation of the change that might arrive because you took a brave step towards the sadness wearing down the being you now hug in decided capacity

And then something seems to take place: Clara Maria melts down and her sadness tones slowly enter the outside of her small self to become expanded in the surrounding atmospheric vacuum before they walk away in vapours of nothing

I feel Maria Clara fully now and she now knows that the moment has passed and that mere minutes of sadness are nothing more than the impossibility of being truly happy without being truly sad

Clara Maria, Maria Clara
You are the beautiful side of sadness

The kissing of the floor

Ana Maria kisses the floor everyday
With such competence and application that it astonishes the gods – even the minor ones who are generally less alert to the great miracles of this earth, used that they are to only keep an eye out for that which comes in noisy interrupting loud manner, in waves of electric and ferocious thunder bolts, or in the acute screams of crows, or still, in pompous honks of insecure Mercedes which pass by, dashing with undignified dignity and hasty finesse

But even these minor gods, otherwise distracted by the big deeds of tall people and impressed by their achievements, even they get taken by the abilities of Ana Maria, Ana Maria who sweeps the floor with such detail and inspection as if it is there in the very crust of our earth that the great miracles are to be found, as if it is there that the great kings of the universe have offered vassalage to other kings and queens making the ladders of the cosmos nothing but an unnecessary paraphernalia that can be dispensed of, for it only serves to make one fall down and break this leg or the other, or worst yet, the spine, that central line full of fundamental medulla which no one cannot do without

Ana Maria kisses the floor and I watch her with awe – surprised by her strength and capacity to love and dedicate herself to the dirt of the lower realm, and with such delicacy, fineness, ingenuity

Ana Maria kisses the floor,
First with her silk hands, then with her long black wavy hair, sensual like no other, and then, as a last gesture of eternal devotion, she sweeps the ground with her entire body, a permanent inspection that cannot escape each cell of her corpse, each touch of her softness, where curves and counter-curves have been designed carefully and in the precise spot of the elongation that her self is, only to keep the boredom out of life and bring men the incantation of eternal drunkards

The princess of Pluto one might call her, trying to help that God of the under-realm control the venom that some beings have brought to this place we call a house, and only sometimes a home, that place we so much need

Ana Maria kisses the floor
With all that she has got

Magnificent shadows

I walk through the shadows rescuing the pieces that I was and that I am

I slip on old newspapers – letters scattered in that wasted sheet of yesterday's happenings, a sheet that was blank, meditating in the possibility that always pulsates before things become what they are and can only be, taking one single stand against the many others that could have been

I feel the members of my being coming to life as I move through the dusty road, a dusty road that could have been – a clean field grass through which I, like a princess, could cavalcade to the encounter of different ways – a dusty road that could have been a wave of water mixed with air as if I were a transcendental surfer that knows how to skip the space between sky and earth, between water and air's apparent emptiness, jumping like a pro to the realm of full existence

But the dusty road is the possibility that I chose, the path that came upon me, as if I, like a fatal marionette, could only do so much to have the illusion of full control over what I am here – or in an unexpected turn, as if the dusty road is in fact the only way that I could have followed with my old and tired feet which have walked and walked many paths, many circular vessels or sometimes simply straight ahead because life is only as neat as we allow its definition to be

And so the dusty road, if you appreciate clear directions, less saturated with the lines of intrusive poetry, the dusty road is in fact a path of many paths, a multiple line with vessels and vessels, with creases and slopes, with ridges and caves concaves, like a true, true enchanting labyrinth of hidden surprises that may not be clean but which are fundamentally our human destiny

And so the dusty road is the multiple artery that I have been walking upon since 1969 – the year that brought me to this station – to this foggy page of terrain that makes fly in the air, the particles that compose my history up to now – this dusty road, this foggy page where I, like an animal running from an invisible hunter, have been leaving marks, the paws of a wild rabbit or a fox printed upon the terrain that takes notice of my existence, and sometimes even blood marks scattered in the most hidden places, screaming like the mirage of my life, the full pulsating vein, the unmistakable print that I am and the vivacious intimation that I have to leave – the mirage of my life or the sure proof that I live and move and get beaten once in a while by hunters of less moral tendencies than those that I, as a young damsel, used to imagine in my unelaborated unawareness of the full dimension of life

Life and the iron bars that impede my voyage through the des-impeded path, to find the end of the road that I envisage to be full of lights and foggy benevolent presences, famished that I am of other ways of being, or still a child in poor imagination who cannot see in the messy dusty road printed in the newspaper until today, the full incantation and dimension of her life

Shattered life, my cells moving through the many circles of this mansion that is really the central station we all walk on – whether we do it on all four, leaving more marks like a baby just starting or whether we stand tall and move firmly in the minutely broken stones and particles that constitute the only gravel that we are and have been – full proofs left there, testimonies that matter really exists, that my own body is heavy and it hurts sometimes, and it smells exuding the only possibility of real and true life – magnificent shadows of what I really am

Dreaming of crosses

I dreamed of crosses and letters and blood
Scattered on the wall of the martyrs of the world
Puzzles and ideas, fast racing cars and profound chanting
music incanted by the burning Joan of Arc – her shaved
head disappearing in the flames of the Inquisition

I dreamed of crosses and letters and blood
And Joan of Arc – and I looking into her inflamed eyes trying
to run but my legs were pinned to the cross of my iron bed
and I – I could not move to the encounter of my medieval
sister – living alone in the fires of the higher priest's inferno

I dreamed of crosses and letters and roses
Roses that I saw after profound meditation, coming out of
Joan of Arc's eyes
The child of medieval times dying for the beauty that
madness allowed

I dreamed of crosses of letters of blood of roses – red roses
white roses
All pinned to the wall of your and my existence
Glimmers of memories that come to me when I am down
– sleeping with the night pigeons and the dusty swallows
– asleep by the luminous dark caves concaving me into
fabulous lines that cover the bottom of the web that sustains
us all whether by night or by day – channel of no end

I dreamed of crosses and letters and roses and blood – the
perfect tableau of our centre of gravity

I dreamed of crosses of letters of roses of you

In the moment

I am in that moment of the morning
Between the zenith of the day and the zenith of the night
Where no one enters to disturb my sense and I only hear
the imperceptible movements of the light coming and
going, coming and going, trying to hold on to this present
immeasurable time, this miracle of the little gods, who give
me so much reason for being, no need for silvering gold
hurting my inner hymen – barely touched by the true lover
of my life

I am in the moment, the moment
Between the zenith of the day and the zenith of the night
The terrain of valleys and curves of peaks and ridges and
slopes
Where the possibility is more than itself – it is in fact

I am in the moment, the moment
Of the middle zenith where nothing can interrupt the
fullness of my feelings
And the completeness of my discoveries – an oriental state
orienting my true self

In the moment,
The zenith of the day and the zenith of the night
Where I am

The idea

I find it in the yellow of the ripe, ripe melon when its sweet water invades my mouth and all my tongue becomes entangled in a feast of sugar and cinnamon of running-s and stopping-s – a seemingly undecided movement that knows how to perform the right tango

Or in the red watermelon when my teeth bite into its soft meat disintegrating it instantaneously – like the goddess of rain does when she unveils the power that inhabits in the dark compact clouds and sends controlled rain, soft and slow, down on us – with an instinctive familiarity, as if I were the garden where it grew to become what I become before I put it into my mouth

I find it in the little seeds of the ready strawberries which almost pass undetected through the channel of my oesophagus – that secret dark valve that is the central cause of the connection between my life and the life of the pulsating outside

Or when I stop and stare with balanced integrity at the peaches that are almost at the right stage of maturity, exhibiting that colour between faint scattered red and eternal golden, golden beige – the orient of my being – orienting the direction that I ought to take to encounter the source of the well, down by the luminous channel, or the windmill with its circular antenna never stopping never stopping

I even see it in the intense red of the blouse the lady standing at the corner of the dark street wears when waiting for her true saviour and waving her body as only a true stubborn fool can do – like a bleeding moving sun under the undying stars of a closed unkind sky

Or in the diffused sore of the vast elephant who, despite his eternal age, still finds it in himself to incubate the breeding of life

The idea is really everywhere

The pulsating of my temporal lobe

The right and the left one – both in sync with that which
lays there in the back paws of my foremost being

The vision or the supra-vision of the true artists of the
world constantly imagining how it is that memory must
be remembered – how it is that the taste of the mud
communicates with my tongue

How it is that sometimes I put my finger on it to feel under
my thumb the vibration of the universe's magnetic wave
in its circular compounding manoeuvres transmitting
the energy from place to place so that all the letters are
transported to the lovers of this world

Transported through reliable, permanent and unforgettable
cadences of musical drums, pastoral symphonies and we
– we are not blind to the great astounding beauty of the
world we see mostly with our eyes closed and our multi-
cellular memory

A memory acutely aware of the important things of this
world that we must take note of
Because we are not blind, we are not blind – as the
pulsating cadence informs me and you every time we put
our fingers to the task

The event of my becoming

I am an o that is not an O
A garden that is not a garden
An egg that is not an egg
A hen that sings like a rooster sometimes, losing her
anonymities and gaining the sense she had been lacking

I sing songs without words that then become words
I paint real flowers at the bottom of myself – in that humid
puddle full of visceral life
Full of visceral becoming

The event of my becoming is grasped when I am fully
asleep involved in incantations of the outer or under world
Or when I run after the wind like a fool of the invisible
Or when I lift up my flowery round skirt and return
drowsy to the circle of my childhood
When everything was beautiful and the whirling waters
were the dancing cascade of my complete being
Or when I scratch the earth and look for the leeches that
have the living blood of my ancestors
Or when I laugh that uncontrollable laugh and everyone
stops to listen to the hollowness that exists in them – the
violin composed of all the strings of the world, weaving and
weaving, the tapestry of our largeness – singing me and you
and them into an undivided line that never ends never ends
blending the unfriendly

The hydrangea of my dreams
The black tulip of my nights and days
The time of the mime without the cutting line

The garden of O that is really an O
The egg of the hen that is really a hen and a rooster too
The insightful song, the morning, awakening me from me
so that I enter you and you and you – the true revelation of
the circular

I am a garden – the garden of O

Friday

Friday is the day of birds
Of swallows and pigeons
Of doves and sparrows
Of starlings too

Friday is when I stop and rest between the back of my
bones and the top of my skin
When I slow down the blood to hear the rivers that run
centrally in me – that walk that slide like newborn dew –
drops that come from above falling feeling in me because
the moon, in her full maternal care, does not forget to bathe
the innocent in waves of lunar cotton and whirls of magic
illusions – the stunning graveyard of a godly circus

Friday is the day of birds – of pigeons and swallows of
sparrows and doves and crows
All dancing in the empty space of the sacred scarce
becoming – that moment when the minister of God
murmurs the palatable sermons of the forever and the
beyond and I see, in slow incanted movement, the spirits
of the Charon, that great moon of Pluto that emits light –
light like no other

Friday is when I lay down in adoration and cry silently
mimicking the yearning of the crows only because I know
that I am being heard – adored by nothing unburdened by
the duty of bread making

Friday is the day of birds and swallows of pigeons and sparrows
Of enchanting crows
When I am

Friday still

Friday is the day reserved for the rewriting, the rewriting of the angels

Between the spaces of the rocks at the beach I inscribe letters that are not so
Between the grains of sand, I procure minutely, like a true blind of eternity, the symbols of the alphabet – I search for letters, the Alpha and the Omega, and that which is between them, hiding in full pulsating desire, under the disguise of a boring tiresome priest of the old who has lost appetite for the feast of the vivacious

I run them all through my tongue, tasting the salt and the potassium required to allow me the balance of the soul and the health of the body, which when perfectly married can perform the magnitude of the unbelievable

I run them all through my tongue, tasting the salt and the potassium of the sea that comes and goes – that leaves and stays – that murmurs and withdraws like a jealous witch or an overly protective mother, who tells but does not tell, enveloping the secret of the treasure in the infinite sounds of the true language

I wave at the waves like an undulating stick trying to become a word – the swords that will incant the impossible, that will cut and sing making me bleed and you too because without the colour of life nothing makes any sense and we only slide, lost and forgotten in the bad taste of the pretentious warlock

Making me bleed and you too, so that joined, we navigate through the broom of flying dreams of snowflakes like the train of the eternal, emitting, in its compassed moment, the transparency of air

Writing for the angels or the Friday of life
The last and biggest day of the working week

Writing for the angels, or the Friday of life
When I wear the golden earring full of inner ridges inside circles
Those that Grandmother Beatriz left for me – as a present to remind me
Of writing, for the angels, or the Fridays of life

I have come from far away

I have come from far away
Far way from who I was
And in search of me I must follow, flow backwards, with
eyes closed and neck elevated
to the line of being

I have come from far away and far and away I must go to be
you and you and you too
In the swirling, whirling sensation of the great water, the
garden of O

I come from far – very far away, away and now I must
deeply concentrate to get away from the smallness that I
have become and enter the circling cascade of the great
luminous channel

I must re-enter and not be afraid of the dark light
For I truly know that the reason is at the very end of the
burning great sun
When the lunar light invades me with educated tenderness
and allows me to shine astronomically, to be able to finally,
fully released, exude the power of being all that I really am

I have come from far away
Very far away
And far way I must go
To enter faraway lands
The true home of my longing

The traveller

I came from a land beyond the setting sun
A land without moons and suns and stars
Inhabited by the luminosity that only darkness can invent

I come from the region of noiseless fountains that flow like
the fly of my legs crossing the space between here and the
point after

I come walking through the night – invisible warlock
transporting the transcendentalism of the roses

I crossed rivers and seas blind to the danger of the full
waves and fierce like a brave and erect black horse, unafraid
of the invisible energies that inhabit the charcoal quilts of
our round universe

I come with the confidence of blind wonders like the prince
of the trans-continental
Flying when possible walking when needed crawling
when demanded floating when dreamed swimming when
required, and permitted by the monsters at sea

I am the man from beyond the circles of light the paths of
roses the laugh of the stars the caves of concave dangers

I am a traveller through the night of being meeting lost
sisters lost brothers
The wandering souls of the many rings that forge the
universe

My garden and yours

I am guided by the subtlety of your movements
When you lay down and I see you, in utter concentration
of myself

I lay there and perceive the distinction of your shallow
respiration and the eucalyptus aroma of your scent –
ephemeral and forever present
That life that takes me into me

I walk backwards slowly but steadily and gradually I see
roses and roses
Endless fields of white and then red and then red and white
mixing in the marriage of the chandelier – the everlasting
hug hanging from there like meadows of spotless life –
like breaths of invisible primal wolves adoring the matron
moon and howling the yearning they have been keeping in
as if afraid of the rude scientists who have taken over their
territory – and desire to vent

Breaths that carry your life and mine – full central mills
where the fire, red and convoluted, runs in constant
mutation to keep the equilibrium of the tower, of the watch
of ticking and tacking over the world

It is my garden and yours and knowing that we simply
dance and stare at the immanence of the scent

The circularity of hydrangeas or the garden of O

My morning comes slow – like a dance of imperceptible movement
Or like the still air of a hot summer afternoon when I simply lay in the dark room peeking through the wide window of my lens that extends all over the sheet that is my skin

It is in this disposition that I enter the garden of hydrangeas where the sun lives in almost dark shades mounting the petals of the plants with slow concentrated manoeuvres
Like a ladybug that in her smallness is nevertheless fully present and aware of the fashion trends as the chic dots of her skin denounce with assurance – fully present and sure of her destiny

I stare at the petals of those hydrangeas – the flowers of my soul – and dance with them
There are many composing the several grapes of the sturdy plant and so I have to sensibly stare my oblivious attention in each and each – here and there – like a sleep of revelation or adoration for the untold

I do that – I am the garden – the garden of O – or a round hydrangea of foolish fresh new tones that turn pale and pale – baby blue – baby yellow – baby rose
Baby – baby – baby – so many that I return to myself to the womb to the moon to the magnified circle

The circularity of hydrangeas or the garden of O

Release

I release my breasts from the gag of the daily chains
I take off my skirt and the inner pants too
Moved by the lightness of movement I slide through the
house

I and my body hang free of all the currents of the modern
world that want to delay the inevitable
Normally, gravity takes hold of me, and I and my body,
kneel down to kiss the humid mud of the earth

I run outside, a free fool not stopped by the laughter of
those who continue to gag their breasts, their legs, their
smiles, their dull phalluses

If they laugh at my boldness I do not hear the sound of
their insecurities
If they point at the drooping effect of my nipples and the
looseness of my skin I wave at them in forgiving adoration

If they whistle the whistle of disapproval I return to
them the transcendent sound of the ancient whistler, the
wise travelling salesman, who comes to visit me in my
nightmares when I, in profound disturbance, cry in refusal
of my decaying body and try in desperation to recompose
its form by mutilating it with toys of the modern world
making my blood dry

I whistle that sound waiting, wanting for them to find
their ancient beautiful memory palpitating with life in the
surface of their dying cells

And then, just when I think that my wish is lost in the vacuity, I am rewarded with a whistle from one of the accusers – that sound that leaves no doubt about the lesson learned

The sound of release like milk dropping down on my chin taking over my entire body making me the bride of the ephemeral Levant – like white butterflies rubbing imperceptible wings against my porous being at the verge of liquid disintegration annihilation – like water waves contained in the circularity of the central lake where murmurs of the eternal are heard and kissed with the caress of the lower lip against the upper lip – *rouge bâton rouge*

In silence
The silence of the white lambs with their dress evading my skin – coming and going – the release of me of you of them

The silence of the fundamental noise entering my hymen – the gem, the stone of my soul
The hymen of the ear
The channels that meet

Finally
In the ultimate play of cards
At the theatre by the bay – where eagles fly and bring the salty smell of the sea and the putrid taste of dead algae

The wideness of flight
That only pure tenderness can allow

The top of my foot

The top of my foot is very white
So white that I can see all the veins spreading through and moving in all directions, linked with each toe

I am always very surprised by it
When my distracted stare comes across my naked feet I marvel at that vine tree that moves me along the world in ways certain and uncertain

I look at the vine leaf intently and imagine the wine, how red it is, how it can make me travel very long distances in a pleasant haze or dusky road, sometimes feeling the world but not feeling, drunkard of the eternal, or in a speedy chase when I feel the danger coming to me and take off to the moon evading the hunting of the cannibal and ascending to the marvellous vacuum where I can swim

The top of my foot is something very strange,
Very intimate
Very beautiful

That is what I think
I think children think the same
For very often a toddler or two will come to me and stare at it, stopping there with astounding surprise as if they have just encountered the reason of life,
The reason that will make them feel the pulse of the land and the velocity of blood

After staring at it, they put it in their mouth sucking it like the breast they have not yet had, and then they laugh with the eagerness of someone who wants to grow up fast and cavalcade the beautiful woods of this planet

The top of my foot is very white
And very vivid
With veins and sub-veins running in all directions to catch the train
Before the last whistle of the hurried conductor

The conductor is thin, and he has a thin moustache
And a frank smile on his face

My body is full of water

My body is full of water
There is so much liquid in me that sometimes I forget how
to take a bath

My body is full of internal murmurs and waves which come
to me in slow cadences or in turbulent Atlantic sea waves
full of salt and debris collected from the movements the
unsteady world makes

My body is heavy sometimes – like a thousand iron
bars weighing upon my back, the metallic bull who does
not know when to stop harassing me because he is fully
immersed in himself and inflamed by the heat of the
moment

My body is a candle of lunar lunar light resting on the back
bone of my being, with all the ribs properly inserted in
its cage, and with all the diaphragms measuring the right
measures so that my organs can breathe the meanderings
of life and spin music through the air waves, reaching the
crickets of the sky and the space beyond the milky galaxy
where the point of no return becomes the point of true
return

My body inflates and deflates like a balloon, like a pregnant
cow, like the anus of the hen when she gives birth to the
perfect round wonder of the world

My body finds music in the dark channels of my throat
where food has gone down and up way too many times to

feed and un-feed the hungry girl that pulsates in the realm
of the black wolf, or to forget the unfaithfulness of life that
does not give, does not forgive, and only wants to rob you
of the abracadabra your grand-mother taught you when
she was young and beautiful and in love with the goats and
the old man who abandoned her for the neatness of clean
sheets and the greenery of large corn fields

My body crawls down in pain when the season reaches me
and I want to eject the life that I am and that could not find
fertility in me – I crawl and howl in utter beautiful pain for
the eternal that I know truly exists and wants to find house,
somewhere, somehow, someday – by the river-lake by the
bay full of birds, by the garden replete with multicolour
hydrangeas crying for the acknowledgment of the birds and
the sting of the bees

I roll it in pieces of white and pink cotton becoming a bride
of softness – clouding your vision and mine
And then when I wake up in the morning I am what I have
never been

The ring of the married happy bride
The pulse of the slow waves of Lake Elias
The tilting of the curtain that slowly becomes alive
And discovers the true importance of light and encounter

I live on top of the world

I live on top of the world
On the wings of clouds when they are dark and heavy
just before they fall on earth and empty the weight of the
universe on the shoulders of suffering beings cleansing
them from eternal sorrows

I live on top of the world
On the wings of sparse and very thin clouds, that fog
of days unsure of what they must be, if compact sheets
descending the night on earth or transparent fleece ready to
adorn the marrying bride

I live there, parading all the land and all the air that your
open mouth aspirates, paying attention to the many
movements that you make, all the sighs you emit when
searching for immaculate snow flakes that only come in the
solstice of winters clean, when December hits time and the
world becomes equal

I live on top of the world
On the moving beaks of doves who fly away escaping from
bad elements
On the tiny feet of starlings who build nests wherever they
can making the entire world the perfect place to be and
grow children

I live on top of the world
Between the lines of light and the lunar night of matron *Lua*
In that space between night and day when the only
catastrophe of life is the particles of silver bullets that

you, in your unclean profession of treacherous thug, let fly above, disturbing the time that is the time and annihilating the cadence of white roses

I live on top of the world
Slowing down the racing of my heart beat, laying in the suspense of the here and the there, of the now and the tomorrow, that interval of non-life – the true actuality of my total being

I live on top of the world
Feeling the currents of the winds of trans-seasons, not missing any midpoint, ending or beginning, like a star of the eternal, or a tulip not sure which colour to emulate and letting the un-sureness fill her with the intensity of the oceanic

I live on top of the world
The perfect house of my choosing

The mountain dweller

I live in the mountains hearing the sounds of muses of the
wonder world coming from the bellies of valleys and the
soul of flowers

Where water and green grass run with the calmness of
things that know time is still,
I live there and sit in silence on the peak of each inflated
belly, that softness that feels like the nipple of my mother's
breast which I remember drinking from with mesmerized
astonished infant gayness

I sit in acute surveillance of the music that comes from
the realms of worms and maybugs, the pianists of
transcendence illuminating my nights and days – the time
of my being when the coin is found and I become conscious
of the range of my wealth

When I am sick of the same position, I lie on my side,
facing the oriental rainbow of daybreak, imagining how
the habitants of Mongolia and other parts of the Levant
may live, how they may espouse the importance of silence
or how they may prefer the noise of imperial grand feats as
long-life brides to kill solitude of the soul and body

And in other days, when loneliness from lack of human
company sits through my bones and makes cold even the
hidden vein of my underbelly, in those days, I crawl like
a snake trying to recuperate the warmth of the volcanic
burning fires that melt the insides of the mountain body

The house without mirrors

I live in a house without mirrors
A complete mansion of darkness, where in order to find
myself, I need to constantly reach for my hand, and touch
the bed and the chair, things other that will remember
my own life, like lights that bring reason to my body and
materiality to my knowing

I spend my days as if they were nights such is the lack of
sight and self-reflection, I scream often to make sure that
I have a voice, that things do come out of my mouth, that
dark channel or never ending road that takes in and expels
like a machine that knows its role in preciseness

I whistle sometimes too, in cadent counted breaths, to
convince myself that I can be a self-reliant pianist, able to
learn from nothing and yet create wonderful slippery arias
that remind you of the eternity of the sea

I wash myself at the window of the back corridor in nights
of full moon to teach my eyes how to look at the roundness
of my body still young and full of eggs that could become
babies, boys or girls, depending on me

I bathe there, in slow, quiet acquiescence receiving the only
light that my house is able to take in

I live in a house without mirrors, an ancient solitary,
running away from her own self,

And so the incumbency that rests upon me is harsh for I have to find very ingenious methods of encountering the evidence of my presence

Sometimes I get tired or very lonely or even terrified that I might be unable to rescue me from me and disappear into nothingness

But I have to be brave, like a child full of miracle who believes in growing up, and in all the fullness that will be found at the end of the line, when all the objectives have been fully met

I have to believe, that I can truly grow up, like the agents of the X-files

I live

I live in the fluid roads of eternity
On the tip of the sun waiting for the gaze of the stars to enhance my days

I live on top of black or white horses barely touching their skin and feeling their animal odour which reminds me of the beautiful uncanny that my life is

I live on scarce fields of ripe grapes, in the nectar of the fruit, all season long, waiting patiently to reach the point of maturity when I will become the taste of your entire body and will feel all your sacred fulfilled insides

I live on top of palm-springs between the water and the palms and the springs of each season of the year

I live hidden in the notes of your voice when you sing your inner song that tells the world about the cadences of the possible beautiful, marks that mark me with letters of long, long remembrances and enhance the colourful dress that I am

I live on top of the highest mountain peaks, singing to the world, in silence, and composing the number that makes your life bearable and your days filled with the emptiness necessary to keep crossing the long road and pass through the harsh winters untouched by darkness

I live in the languages that exist in each country of the earth, in the singing clicks of Xhosa, in the wide breathless vowels of the Portuguese verbs when they are composed in the imperfect past making time just complete and filled with awe, without disjunctions or conjunctions, in the harsh sounds of Russian when Vladimir sings a song of Perestroika, in the romantic poetry of French when Baudelaire and Verlaine enter my wide vein and I become, I become, melting on the floor and existing with the *chora*

In the clean sounds of the English language which comes to me with the sharpness of precise arrows that hit my mind and clarify the thought that I did not know existed before I learned this tongue, in the word "Amore" that exists and announces itself in slight variations in all the romance languages allowing me to dream the undreamed and shiver of musical incantations, vocal secrets vibrating through each of my cells and multiplying the piano that my entire body is

In the Spanish singing ways that bring the wonders of Don Quixote to a visible possible trajectory plane, placing them right in front of me, and allowing me to grab the magic of the crystal glass when I enter the house of the lord and become an un-suffering Christ-ess whose destiny is not to die but live through the eternity of transparent light, permanently staring at the beautiful wide universe and entering the gargling cascade of life, the circular foundation that runs without destiny, because everything is everywhere and water knows no boundaries so malleable that it is

I live in the Chinese characters, in their intricate complexity, which perplexes me without end, until I forget who I am only to remember myself better in the strange that there stares, or in the longing beautiful song that the Arabic language is, and which reminds me of my own Lusitanian language and the *fado* that it sings with the eternal crying voice of a hurt elephant, mourning and mourning for Allah in every call to prayer, at the top of the blue and white mosque, early, early in the night, before God has even sent another of his creations down on us, which you must take with hands open, take and use to create the wonderful so that you may realize godliness

And I live on all the other languages that I can't even describe with a simple and poor metaphor so distant are they from my hearing ear, I live in their absence from me, in their unreachable sounds that I imagine when I lay distracted on the grass on a very hot summer day, or when I spend time with my baby niece and she babbles into me my lost tongues, awakening me to some possible communication with the speakers of other syllables

Living still

I live on the tip of the morning song of the king rooster
when he brazes the freshness and silence of the morning
dew with the urgent cry of visceral life

I live in the shadows of my nails and on their white spots
too that might indicate that the calcium that is in me is
running out of ink and that I need more milk, milk from
cows and goats that graze on clean green grass untouched
by nothing

I live on top of rain drops in that space that makes
me round like a perfect pearl, the one carrying the
transcendentality of my liquid eyes

I live on the thin lines that write themselves in my face
and neck as my skin ages and takes refuge into the sublime
annihilation that death is

I live on the black rings of Mexican wasps, in the sweet
juice that has been gathered from the heart of flowers and
waits in limbo for the moment when honey just happens

I live in the smoke that comes out of my chimney in
winters cold when the knowledge of my body is the most
important to take note of because trembling becomes a
response to the fundamentals of existence

I live in holes on the ground entering the houses of crickets
and becoming versed with the organ music that flows from

the earth's core upwards so that you and your neighbours
can formulate the eternal and stare at the aria superior

I live on scattered and scarce trees that lay existent in the
Kalahari Desert of Namibia becoming myself too and
realizing the aqua marina of my real reflection

I live on the veins of maple leaf trees, on the three perfectly
designed valleys that become yellow and then red and then
brown before they disintegrate in the full nothingness of
being and realize their potentiality of life

I live on the screams of the pig when he dies under the
knife of the butchers of my village who are hungry and
poor and educated peasants who need blood to keep theirs
running

I live in the bells of my goats when I take the profession
of goatherdess, a Queen able to hear the musical realms of
unicorn beings that do not recognize national borders and
become announcements of the crosscurrents

I live on the tip of my toes constantly walking on eggshells
afraid to disturb the babies who sleep in the bedroom at
the corner of the house, which is the most silent part of the
mansion unperturbed by the banalities of life

I live between words and syllables that say nothing and wait
vacant in the possibility of meaning

I live on the red tiles that cover up my house keeping out
the elements that are prejudicial to my health, and by doing
this important job I am given the privilege of feeling the
clean sensibility of snow when it falls down upon me and
makes the roof that I am a home for all of us

I live on your dead skin cells, in that state between your
being and non-being, incanted by the middle space of the
"yes" and the "no"

I live in the bubbles of foam that come from your lavender
soap, inhaling the scents of all the plants belonging to that
sacred family, *Lavandula Officinalis*

I live in the transdisciplinary fields, between French and
English, side by side with Greek and Portuguese, on top
of Latin, in the slight dream of Iroquois, in the metonyms
and metaphors, in the *mise-en-abîme* of *mises-en-abîme* of
languages trying to reach the exteriority of tongues

I live in the written and unwritten, in the imagined,
the envisioned or envisaged, in the palpable and the
untouchable, in the zones of un-zones, in the barely
bearable, in the possibility of the impossible, the lightness
of darkness, the closed proteas of South Africa or its
waiting to happen jacarandas

Living again

I live on top of the sun, behind the amber of the galactic translucent black holes, in the synchronism of invisible tango dances that enchant me in perfect rhythm, taking my bones to the beginning of the world incident when time ceased to be and my self and yours became shattered by the noisy passing of shoes produced by the dozen in factory lines of my life and yours

I live in the howl of the midnight cat when he calls for her in vain for hours and hours because she is very far away and cannot hear his crying for God

I live in the backbones of dead elephants which lay open under the scorching sun on the wide plains of the Great and Little Karoo, waiting eternally to become invisible ashes and merge with the dusty soil entering the muddy realm of abundance

I live in the roots of your very dark hair in the space that links your outside with your inside making you whole – an angel of the perfect universe

I live on the cancerous cells that have taken over my sister's breasts and the bone marrow of my long gone dear friend Isabel who is nothing now, no more than the pollen of life, Isabel who went away in that sullen November Fall, leaving me stranded by the bay with the remembrances of both of our lives weighing on my single shoulders

I live in the life and death that life is, in the ugly and the beautiful of rotting cellars, of purple tulips, of magnified magnificent hydrangeas

In the blood that I suck from my index finger when I cut onions for my soup and become blind because I am afflicted by the tears of plants that have to die constantly to feed the ethical egocentric self of humans who think themselves more committed to the philosophy of respect for others, forgetting that otherness is everywhere and escaping it would be to escape ourselves and become the other that I now eat

I live on the line of clean clothes when I put them outside in the open field and stare at them waving under the wind of being, feeling the labour of my hands, still red and wrinkled from the cold water of the running river down by the hanging meadow of Mountain Meya, where I knelt down in adoration

I live on the casting eyes of butterflies, in the retina that knows when spring is coming and when the wind is favourable to medium flight, that perfect place from where to see the world

I live on the air waves of cell phones, in the voices that you transport to me when you are far away on a business trip and think of sending messages from the underground so that my large vein can keep alive and fully red, an open beautiful life wound exhaling the perfume of true love that always remembers

I live on scarce and very meagre pieces of bread, not because I am poor but because in my vain fraternity with the truly destitute, I want to imagine the taste of hunger and the coldness of the body

I live in the smallest waves of the Atlantic ocean, the ones that only the careful onlookers can detect, or on the floating algae that exists near the beach where the children gather to play fools and become acquainted with the fluidity of the sand and the lunar light that descends at night making the sea the Queen of Sheba dressed in platinum royalties, the card with unlimited credit, and the only one you will ever need to buy all the wealth of this world

I live in the humidity of the deep valleys of the Northern Hemisphere, where sheep keep their faces close to the ground to savour the milk of God and goats stay low too resisting the urge to mount the mountains and stare at the divine from above

Or on the lush green parts of the Amazonian great forest with creatures of all millennia staring at me in tenderness, even the Anaconda snake which is often accused of cannibalistic acts in the popular movies made to indulge and lie to the innocent or misinformed

I live on the brave birds that gather on top of the great Buffalo to eat the annoying parasites that keep bothering the big animal, or the belly of disgusting cockroaches where the dirt of the world gathers in remembrance of good and evil, or the puddle of stale water on the middle of the open field, tasting the smell of that which is only to arrive when the condition of the ugly and the beautiful is everywhere – the sheet of the inseparable twins without which we cannot do

I live on top of myself, a sister in awe outside my body only to arrive early at the reign of God and have more time with

the angels or to know myself better because sometimes
the ones at the window of the mansion become the true
chevaliers, the truly informed who are able to bring all the
news to the house, thus filling the void with the sense of
the great dark light or the rats of the underground

Do not be disappointed with the seemingly strange mixture
of metaphors I use to explain to you the true nature of the
home where I live

Because the ugly and the beautiful are inseparable siblings
who make being what it can only be:

Perfect

The feeling of the frog

The frog is not what you think it is
It is also not what I am about to tell you using the best metaphors I can think of
But hopefully, and if you are in a non-personal disposition, the idea of the frog can be found in very slight hopes, at the borders of the words I will be using, above the "R" and below the "F", on top of the "O" and just side by side with the "G"

The frog is green and yellow and brown too, a creature, a being, whose colour I cannot completely see under the light that I am using and the shadow affecting my senses

The animal is uncanny, living on land and in muddy ponds full of watery plants which like "it" do not want to belong to either world only to belong to both more fully – perhaps

I used to play with the frog when I was a child, and sometimes not in such a nice manner, for in my intolerable boredom, I needed to find toys in a land where none were given to me by the adults of my life

In my need to understand otherness and get out of my self, I would hurt those little amphibian animals with crude and raw delight only to stare at their dead life after my abominable act

They looked like toads but were not such since they needed more water, they were neither one thing nor the other but

I could see in them particles of fishes and remembrances of cobras, yet they were neither one nor the other

They were themselves, individual makings that did not want to appear to my eyes in a clear dissected manner, lovers of transcendental discoveries

And so, in my malevolent childish ways, that demanded responses to all the "whys" of this world I was pushed to destroy their life and stare at their inner entrails which also did not reveal me more

And so, I was left alone in my self, as I always had been, and thus not satisfied and still more adventurous and devilish I would take a last step:

I would pick up the mass of the thing that was now lifeless on the floor of the earth's crust with my bare hands, and I would feel its coldness against my own closed palm and at that moment I seemed to feel a little glimpse of the life of the corpse – as if my own body was now in my own hand and being there, I could understand myself just a tiny little better

Black magnolias

Yesterday I had a dream
Of black magnolias
Those flowers of life appeared to me in their full rare black enchantment, like princesses of the Dark Continent, where pearls of very high category can be found, and where the genetic line of all humanity has been encountered or so say the latest scientists who are experts in the life of old bones

Yesterday I dreamt of black magnolias, roses and roses of staring ministerial beauty coming to my encounter to tell me the news of the underworld and remind me of the powers of the unvoiced

I woke up this morning and looked around my room for their presence – the idea of their idea, and to my surprise, I found them everywhere:

In the angular corners, where usually, I would only see the collected dust of the unbearable passing of the time, in the vases of plastic flowers on top of the desk put there to remind me of the impossibility of freezing beauty

On top of the old book that smells like a five hundred year old bible waiting to be opened so that it can tell you the miracles of Jesus and those of St. John the Baptist who baptized the former and survived the scorching desert eating the life of innocent crickets that were also creatures of God

On the white paintings hanging from the white wall which
tell a mute story about the convention of the Mexican
bees at the back garden of the house and the fighting of
the hungry mice on the underground floor of the mansion
where I lay

On the hanging old chandelier the colour of purple that my
great-great-grandmother inherited from her great-great-
grandmother and then passed on to me to keep the family
river running towards its unmistakable destiny

On top of the only bedside table that I have in my room, in
its crevices that were once a very old oak tree planted at the
big plaza by the central garden of an old town, so old that
I have numbed its name in some part of myself that now
remains unreachable so sleepy it has become

I also see its intention on the thick coloured cotton quilt
covering my single bed and body keeping me from getting
sick and unable to dream

The black magnolia has entered my house

Imagining sorrow

The time of Saturday and Sunday is the worst time of what time means

After the illusion of a friendship I had with a female who then exchanged me for the warmth of a companion of the opposite sex, and as usual, I rest alone again, in the silence of a house that thumps with music sometimes, but not always, because always is really an eternity too difficult to bear alone, without not losing oneself from time to time

After days and days of loosening myself with her, the friend that I had before she fell again for the friendship that will make her complete, at least for sometime, after that light gayness of days, I return to me in isolation and ponder upon why people must love and then let love go, why they must do it again and again, why they can't rest on the same nest for the remaining of their time on earth and avoid suffering and the gargling of blood

Sitting inside a house that could be full but is empty, except for the sounds of music that I hear from outside, played by university students who insist on learning the prize of being important

Sitting there and listening to the games they play while learning how to become savvy in the architecture of pleasure, I feel already the emptiness that is awaiting them, the desolation of an idea that will not reveal itself when it ought to, the house without the necessary structure, the required sturdiness, I listen to that pre-announcement

of the announcement, the noise of the fall of the sublime
mansion that never really took image, I sit there and I feel,
and I get angry at them who make me feel their burden,
like inconsiderate children, full of self-righteousness

I feel that burden, apart from my very own, even though I
have passed the age of follies and have somewhat learned
how to live content with the bareness of life – but not
today, for today I feel the weight of that bareness upon
me and imagine what could be the feeling of a baby in my
arms, the voice of a true lover who could really give it to me
to erase the chains of my isolated self and expand my cells
to the wings of the universe

The middle of the road

Secrets to walk upon
My feet think of the road full of mud and living beings as
offers from the days when the saints crossed the wet rivers
to sprinkle rain upon the grass

I stand still for moments – enough to see the air
intertwined with pollen and broken wings of exhausted
butterflies or sometimes even petals of lost lilac roses which
have left the road below to find incantation through the
sounds discernible when two birds make love and perform
the usual singing ritual thereafter

I meditate the road still ahead afraid perhaps of the
unknown edges that my naked feet might have to stumble
upon so hard can life on this earth be sometimes

I carve designs on the floor with my little toes, the fingers
of the feet and, when in trouble, I summon the help of the
little fingers of the hands, which I have long ago baptized
as the children of God, for they bring much gayness and
tenderness to the time of being among adults

I wave my arms up and down or sometimes in half or full
circles like a truck that has lost direction or is dangerously
low in gas

I whistle in slow, highly controlled breaths to call upon the
music that inhabits in the bellies of maybugs waiting to
hear the complex cacophony of their musical tones and the
yellowish light that emanates secrets of the untold world,

down under the crust of the circuitous realm that can make
me dizzy if I am distracted by the life of the above

I pray the rosary ten times, slowing down before the creed
announces itself, and attaining velocity when I enter the
holy cross that calls the name of the father, the spirit and
the son, and then rests in the wide cavity that is the chest
of the milky mother in full reason for breastfeeding – a
pure matron of this earth not forgetting that her job is to
bring sweets to the wide-eyed children awaiting for the
marvellous train and the news it travels

I jump up and down to exercise the intricacy of my body
and mind until I breathe heavily and my blood runs
red and speedy through the trees and all its branches
that compose the forest that I am from top to bottom,
decorating my life with the force of the spring and the
waves of the sea

I play skip and skip the uneven ridges of the mountains
preferring the refuge of low valleys where the lilacs of the
hills have also found solace from the noisy wind and time
to pray with moles

I walk further and further now that I have incubated
strength and took rest from the heavy and hard exercise of
life

I masticate wild flowers, first separately, one by one, to
taste the flavours of each and the enigmas the bees have
imprinted there while doing their fundamental job of
gathering liquors to produce honey, and after the individual
feast, I put all in my mouth to encounter the collective soul
and evade the fragmented ego

I could do more but for today it is enough, sufficient to carry me through the few next days – and after that, there are always other possibilities

The miracle of the round pot

I cook in the round ceramic pot
I make delicious meals that then enter my body and remind
me that I am round too like the pot I cook in

That reminder is enough to make me enter distances on
the wings of stars and the eyes of the sun – and sometimes
I even fall into the bright holes that populate the cosmic
vacuum where there is nothing but light upon light upon
light, like a river of immanence or the walking of young
babies who still believe in clouds of cotton that can sustain
their weight

I cook so many meals in this round pot and I enter so
many of them, that sometimes I cannot find any distinction
between the pot, myself and the food that I ingest

The pot is me, I am the pot, the food cooked in the pot is
the pot and the pot is the food it cooks

And so the food is me, I am the food, the food is the pot
and I am the pot too

The threesome of transcendence: consubstantiation –
transubstantiation – insubstantiation

The perception of colours

My perception varies vastly from day to day
From moment of the day to another moment of day

When sleeping the siesta of burning afternoons, I can see the shades in an almost clearer manner than when I am with eyes wide open staring at the pencils my neighbour uses to paint his shades and imprint his perceptions of the seasons

In fact, I often prefer to evade the gay brightness of shades to reminisce about the grey areas of the sun and see if I can find spots of untold stories there, stories that tell me about the bees of Africa, the frogs of Mexico, the horses of the dry deserts of the beautiful-sad Mongolia

In the colours of my low perception I can rescue cats from butcher artists who think that the act of killing others is indeed matter to rejoice upon and will merit prizes for innovation in sublime thought and artistic eureka – when it's nothing more than the bad *chora*, the ugly abject of inconscience

In the shades of dark nights I can envisage the waves of the Black Sea, and then, in a magic fast somersault, I can make the Red Sea available to my right retina where seeing is more than staring – it is in fact seeing before seeing – like Lévinas has said, in a slightly different manner, respective to his own transcendence

In the black concave crevices of transparent glasses full of colourful Martinis and green-green olives prepared to bring vision to the vain and bored of life, I can devise brave *cavaleiros* of the distant Dark and Middle Ages, speedy and energetic horseman who run like arrows to the encounter of the enemy and the rescuing of enchanted Moorish princesses – *princesas encantadas*

In the perception of my colours, I walk slow and in dark alleys, only to arrive at the scintillating quality of the faraway star that lives in the untold realms of lightness, so distant it is from the darkness we live in

The perception of my colours is low
And I prefer it like that

Praying the rosary

I pray the rosary for Mary and Joseph and the little boy
they had under the difficult circumstances that many of
us know by reading and hearing about it through the long
centuries of time

I pray it for Dulce who is sick and suffers from lack of the
fundamental vitamins of life: salt, sugar and cinnamon

I pray it for the idea of Nelson Mandela and the childish
persistence of Bishop Desmond Tutu who moves his hands
and his body in circular realms of assuredness and giggles
like a boy in pre-adolescent puberty when the raging
hormones are not yet at work

I pray it for the rainbow to show between the lines of
the sun and the rain when one is neither here nor there
but knows that that state is in itself full of the important
cadences of life rhythm

I circulate it around my ten fingers professing each syllable
of the mystery with the attitude of an assured priest saying
the mass in his best days

I roll it around my tongue so that it becomes more circular
than ever, and I make sure that not one bead is missed,
profoundly incanting the secrets it carries in its ancient
wood which could be oak or chestnut or cherry or plum
– and, in doing so, I can envisage the ripe smell of all the
fruits when they attain the summer full, feeding all those in
need and there are many

I caress the silver cross and I think how its coldness must
have been so unbearable to the one who stood there
bleeding the love of life for all the world to see and learn
from the abhorrent-beautiful scene, the beautiful abject

The mountain pianist

That he chooses such a place to play the organ should not be the surprising factor of what I am about to tell you

That he gets up very early, before anyone else because no one has ever seen him rolling out of bed and putting on his clothes, should also not be a matter for astonishment

That he has a shaven head where the brilliance of his cranium can be seen night and day, and a long, long beard and moustache is also not the highlight of the words I want to weave here to tell you something, something that will remain with you for the long times to come (or so I am hoping)

What I want to imprint and leave inscribed in you is the following:

When he plays the piano (which is always) and if you are really listening, you will be capable of hearing the cedars of Lebanon and the flowers of blossoming equatorial trees, which may appear to you (if you are from the Northern Hemisphere) as strange announcements of utter beauty

When he moves his agile ten fingers through the board of his organ (which is always) and if you are really attentive to the notes that he manipulates, you may be able to feel like a white butterfly moving through the spaces of the moons and the countless galaxies that there exist in that which we cannot see

When he resonates the voice of the music that he creates and then shares it with you (if you are really listening) you will be able to gaze at nothing and in so doing, you may, I assure you, rest in peace in the feathers of the back universe, where nothing and everything are sisters of long time acquaintance

When he walks upon your ears as if nothing, nothing else mattered, and you do not resist the seemingly abrupt interruption of an annoying presence, you my very well be able to feel the highest note of the universe, and you will do so through the very cord that you are, which is nothing short of a true miracle, because you are becoming the vessel through which Being announces itself, and thus no longer alone you are

The mountain pianist is a miracle
Let it announce itself to you

The morning dew

The morning dew is freshly cold, an announcement from the night that has just passed but left its mark, a possible reminder that novelty is within all of us and that we only need to spend time alone to see its intention and capacity

The morning dew is the drop of glory left by the passing stars on their way to other skies where they will also announce the vast possibilities of existence and the concreteness of the truly transparent

The morning dew is the idea that the moon had and then left diffused on the earth so that she does not forget and will be able to pick up on in her next visit, which gradually will become a full circle of notification

The morning dew is the rosary prayed all night long by the millions of souls in the utter darkness, the beads that after so much incantation become pure pearls of divine wisdom, crystal balls where the cleared future can be devised, a statement that forgiveness and miracles do indeed happen

The morning dew is the fresh bath that my naked feet welcome after being quietly asleep for so long in the warmth of a clear, dreamless night, or the holy water through which my hands are able to enter the baptismal tank to receive their true name

The morning dew is the wine of the Gods carried through the night from the Greek and Roman cellars just so that I can have a feast and become the happy bride of Dionysius – that God of Antiquity whose passion never fades

The morning dew is my wedding dress spread like a quilt on the body of the earth waiting in awe and fresh coolness for the groom to arrive so that the beautiful ceremony can proceed

It is my fingers and my toes, my eyes and my mouth, and each cell of my body waiting like apples in the open field, waiting to be picked up and savoured with the slowness of eternity and the cadence of the low waves of the sea, when all is resolved and the winds have found their balance by conversing in secret after dark fell upon the empty space, where sometimes they do create havoc like devilish children unsatisfied with the stillness of life

The morning dew is the eggs laid by thousands of antique hens who arrived in the darkness of the night and left before clarity took over and yet they were able to leave the transcendentality of their wisdom spread all over the land – the incomparable layout that makes the earth the place to be, to call home, and conduct all the rituals that make us divine: the baptisms, the marriages and the mass with the sacred communion – for those of this religion

It is the golden mines that have not been mined and will never be because their bottom lies upside down – on the abode of the earth – and that confuses the gold diggers making them drowsy and incapable of exploring the un-explorable

It is the insularity of time and the remembrance that
humidity exists all over the universe and comes visiting
most nights so that we do not forget our relation with the
faraway

It is me and you – when we step out of the bath, dripping
like newborns, ready to be hugged by the towel of life

The story of the old woman

She is neither a man nor a woman but possesses in her the rich blood line
She is old, very old, almost incapable of walking straight, like a crawling snake that knows all the secrets of the low land and all the roads and paths to the cities of gold and the lakes of silver

She has long platinum pepper hair, pure white-greyish and pure black, a perfecting condiment capable of making the best fish soup and the most savoury Indian curry dish, if you take into account the selection of all the other necessary condiments too of course, because food needs many workers: the cooks and the farmers, the birds and the cows, the pollinating bees and the rains of the sky ...

She dresses in black always, as if she does not want to be seen by night or day passengers because she truly believes black is the nether colour which allows you to stand still and still stand for hours on end without moving one single iris and emitting a single breath – as if death is really there and death is where one wants to be, so peaceful is the coffin where we lay unnoticed by nothing in the black dress of repose

She speaks in loud boisterous gargles of laughter that are nothing but mixed announcements of the ugly and the beautiful – the middle ground of life that allows all of us to see the beautiful face of sadness – like Maria Clara, Clara Maria, whom you already know by name and motive

She bathes in rivers cold and lakes warm, naked, for all to see and stare at, her dripping breasts and lining wrinkles making her a mountain of profound, unending ridges and creases where one might lose oneself only to find the end line and win the race

She peeks at you with uncandid eyes, dark like no other, and you become scared of the intensity that there lives, but after a while you come to love that stare, and you yourself, start staring like that at the other others that may surround you at the time of this event

She dances convoluted dances sometimes, like a drowsy butterfly who has passed her time and forgotten her moves, yet wants to recall immanence to the present of her body and mind, because, thinks she, old is only what you allow it to be, and life announces itself in many dresses, the dark and the white, the twisted and the straight, the coloured and the dormant shade, the ugly and the beautiful, as already said

The old woman scares you and enchants you: like a princess of the dangerous faraway who possesses in her the familiarity of your intimate self, like a witch wearing a certain poise that seduces your need for the uncanny and your attraction to the abysmal

She is the periodic table and in her you find all the necessary elements that make up life: the good and the bad, the poisonous and the healing, the fiery and the noble, the atomic and the peaceful, the smelling and the odourless, the heavy and the light, the visible and the invisible: the Semi-conductors, the Non-metals, the Inert gases and the Lanthanides en actinides – and they all existed long before *Mendeleev* organized them in his scheme

And sometimes her long hair is so stubborn and powerful that it picks up on everything standing on the surface of the earth, or even that which lies above and beyond: the stones and the trees, the running rabbits and the singing cockerels, the eyes of gay Marta Magda or those of sad Maria Clara, the tiny feet of little boys and girls, the petals of dahlias and red roses, the sea algae and the colourful fish, the scent of fresh cow dung, the sensation of the burning sun left on spring young leaves full of chlorophyll, the dust dancing in the air or the dying pieces of fall oaks, the parts of shooting stars that come down from their preferred living place, the darkness of the immense firmament, the moon in its full or imperfect state of being, the lost birds who are not sure of the direction to follow to find spring again – this and much, much more ...

She does all this and the much more that I could not name, and in so doing, she becomes a ball of impossible proportions, a dancing monstrous entity, between earth and sky, like a levitating bride, or the true daughter of the ugly and the beautiful – and faced with the spectacle that she is, you cannot help it: you stare at her like a medium in the middle of his trance seeing with the eye of the Mind, and you cry long cries, prolonged never-ending notes of sadness and gayness, because you have discovered the power that sustains It and makes you the distended thing that you are·

The human settlement

The condition is made
After years of transient humanity the king announces the truth, the beautiful one:

"One shall no longer live separate from our neighbour, one shall forgive and forget, even those who have the wounds raw like open pools of blood where they can still see the bodies of their beloved ones cut in pieces swimming in the floor of hate – crumbles of rotten bread waiting for the bad birds to commit the last abominable act. Even those, must forgive and forget, because life demands that sacrifice, because in the end there will be the reward of us and them finally meeting at the crossroads of sand, where we will become intertwined and lost in one another, true lovers of the eternal hug."

So thus he spoke – the beautiful Zarathustra of our recent times who had in him the grand idea.

I entered his idea – the new country frontier, years later after his predicament and decisive intimation, and saw, in profound disappointment, that it had not yet happened, the beautiful one had not yet been born. I saw it and cried like a child in complete degraded state, a child who had utterly believed that the end, when everything had been done, would bring the most beautiful toy, the one she always thought existed even if hidden under layers and layers of thick dirty mud, beneath the repellent malevolent cells of human men and women, beings who were in reality just hurting from ignorance, from not being able to take that long cleansing bath that can make visible the glitter of true glitterati.

I saw it – almost like it had been in the old days, only perhaps wearing now a different skirt made with the modern polishing liquid, showing the effects of more intricate factories that despite the knowledge that they have that the environment is dangerously being affected, despite that very knowledge, they keep emitting the fumes thick and compact where no window of light can be divined.

I saw it like that and I yearned and yearned for the beautiful one that was not yet born in the modern human settlement of the new South Africa.

I saw it and I summoned the angels, in conviction for the true revelation of the jacarandas, because the child that I still was thought that perhaps the time had not yet come, that the end of the line was still far, far from the objectives that we had set for ourselves

Healing again, Or the dream of South Africa

Healing,
Between my fingers and in the back of my bones
Or in the cells that have fallen and are now gradually trying to recover from the rupture of life – but I should not give into despair for they say it takes seven years for your body to completely regenerate itself and start anew like a baby just born opening itself again to the slow incantations that life may allow

In the presence of sorrow, I am obliged to kneel down again
And remember the chaos that love and profound hurt can cause

I lay open to nothing on top of my single bed, exhausted after a very hard workout at Planet Fitness – the place where I go often to chase away the heaviness of your remembrance in me, which has taken over my thin body and now I am left with a thousand pounds on my back – eternal slave of the world like you think you are – a victim victimizing itself permanently thinking that is the road to justice to salvation to remuneration – what happened to the true forgiving and forgetting that the optimist child-like Bishop Desmond Tutu had in his beautiful mind, and myself too like I told you? What happened to the forced separation to the congregation to the realization to the future to the dream? I am afraid you are afraid? Why? I am hurt you are hurt and we hurt again? Why? I seal myself you seal yourself, you scream, I scream and nobody heals? Why? – the river has to run to cry for many days and years before the healing can come, some say – don't expect miracles of a-human proportions in the land of hurt where hurt has hurt for centuries and centuries – hear the echoes in the Karoo, in the Eastern and Western Cape, the screaming souls brought by the wind every season of the year

I lay there in my single bed depleted of all the water that I sweated out of my body, a body that has seen many punishments – and not just the ones inflicted by you for even before I met you, I had already reduced its natural, beautiful and plump size, the size my progenitors gave me voluntarily and without intrusion of pre-assigned paradigms, I had already reduced it by doing abominable sacrileges, so abominable that they would make the little gods cry (and perhaps even the big ones, generally used to take notice of greater and more important human disasters)

I lay there hearing the heat that floats outside, between the imagined humidity of the ground and the possible breeze of the sky, I lay like that inside my permanently closed dark navy blue curtains which for the grace of God seal me off from the deadly scorching intrusion that can invade the sanctuary that I need to build to take rest from all my affairs and yours too – because you, in your blindness, in your un-thought crude hurt, made sure to pass some of them on to me

Laying there I note the walls and the corners of the room and I can see lots of dragons sometimes – some exhausted, some vividly engaged in the fight with their enemy who has open long tongues that seem at points to extend from one corner to all the others, making my room (which is my cathedral of repose) a place infested with too much heaviness, too much blood – unbearable loud screams that perturb my time when I try to lie very still to re-encounter that which I have lost

In those moments I am obliged to produce stronger efforts breathings incantations to the little and big gods, including the saints (male and female), the angels and the archangels and all the pagan divinities

I make appeal to all of them so that the corners of my room become less invaded with unbearable presences and, at least for a moment, I can dance in the valley of nothing, where all is clean and the ascent to the mountains is much more than a distant possibility – it is in fact a very possible theory that can take wings and march to the peak of existence – where nothing is but everything and it is there glancing, dancing at you in the happy and resolute chaos of the sky and earth

It is a moment already repeated by my mother, my mother who once said to the police who did not want her to sell cheese on the corner of the road anymore, the corner where she had been selling for more than half a century trying to feed her large family: "My lord, where am I from, you ask? I am from earth and sky, the citizen of large dwellings."

I am healing,
In the back of my bones and in all the spaces that separate each of my fingers
And also my toes
Because my body is mine and it is an entire connected thing unbroken by nothing, a thing that refuses dissection – even in the face of this blind harsh fall it now suffers from

The station of the central

The train stops there, every minute of time, even if you and I, the dormant passengers of life, cannot feel the halting discernible movement of the screeching wheels on the iron strong rails that forge the directions of life

The station, where the train stops every minute, is central, central to the way that I will take in my long walk upon the road that my life is, and it is the same for you: your main point of adjustment to quickly think about that which you must do to get at the place that you need to arrive at

The boys and the girls travelling in the train that stops every minute are noisy and inconsiderate, almost like unsettling irritating birds who must giggle at each object that they see as the train moves through the lines, novelties to their junior eyes which still need to learn how many rosaries it takes to pray to earn the right to divinity, or sometimes they giggle strident mocking sounds, like unkind un-bred beings, and they do so especially when they look at the handicapped dirty passengers of life, the vagrants that stand still at the central station, which is every station, at least for one or two of the people travelling in the train

And on days when it rains a lot, or when the sun is hot like a burning inferno kept alive by men with invisible horns, in those days, the young boys and girls laugh their unkind laughter even more, for hours on end, for they look at the many more vagrants that stand there impeded by the temporal conditions, like lines and lines of lost couriers who either forgot what they were delivering to the VIP, or lost the precious object that they were carrying which was given to them with very specific instructions, they lost it, and now must suffer and be suffocated by the imagined fear of the big boss who surely will not want to pay them their full salary, yes because packages are expensive and there is also the cost of travelling with them on the train, the train that stops every minute at the station of the central – central at least for one or two people travelling in the carriages

They look at them and cannot comprehend their dumb-like gaze of zombies and so they laugh and laugh at the confusion and misery of the vagrants frozen at train stations because they no longer can face the race that life is, they laugh because they are young and do not yet know what it is to feel so tired that one forgets the very reason why one is running and what it is that really stares at the end of the rail road

Sometimes, if I am not that tired myself, and can still find eagerness to note the vagrants of the stations and the children laughing at them, at those times, I look at all of them through the transparent filter that my eye sheet carries and I experience a profound joy and capacity – a capacity to feel the loss of the vagrants and the laughter of the innocent children, I feel that and I cry with water that comes to my eyes through the river golden lake of possible redemption – and sometimes I even get out of my train stepping into a central station, which I know for sure not to be mine, and give them a hand or ask them a question that may help clarify something, something related to their thereabouts and their wheres-to-go

But sometimes it affects me too, so much so that I fall asleep in the train and miss the many stations and the many vagrants and the many children, and in so doing, I become the lost vagrants and the laughing children – I am the train or the station, not the central but just any one of them – and there are so many, so many that I fail to distinguish between the several signs painted on white faded wood, hanging loosely on the walls of the platforms, signs that are mixed with the heat or the rain and the vagabonds and the children and even the sharp whistle of the conductor's helper

Yes because travelling alone and carrying upon one's shoulders the sole responsibility of waking up all the passengers must be a job that no conductor willingly consents to – even if he is sure, sure like a black perfect stallion galloping without hesitation to the finishing line

The intimacy of love

In it there is something, it is a something that makes life bearable and gives sense to the reasons why sunset and sunrise take place

There is breathing, shallow like the rubbing of imperceptible butterflies moving between the zones of the black holes and the lines of the sub-moons of Uranus and Pluto

I see it in the air, moving inside travelling trains, affecting people in an utter state of dream, trespassing zones of sub-zones to lie between the impeding shadows of dark-light terrains where doves fly in circles and sparrows sing lullabies to the soul of children and the vastness of oceans

Or in those perfect moments: the ones that give consolation without previous cause

The intimacy of love is my goal – my ultimate grace where memories of laughter dance in the faces of men and women – my companions for life

Its life walks in the light glimmers of your blue eyes or in the trembling hands that touch my body to remind me that I do exist and that my existence is fundamentally dependant on your body in mine – it is then that my self resembles who she is and rejoices in the pure juice of peach washing down on my throat and allowing me to produce gargles of pristine laughter – the very idea of the one who knows she is alive and breathes the memory of life because of the other

The intimacy of love is you and me meeting – truly meeting at the crossroads of each other – the point of the perfect forest before we enter each other, that garden of scent that makes greenness of tall pine trees the most important gods producing shadows that become the abode we need to fulfil our destiny and find pearls and secrets of the untold under the moss – or play hide and seek between the ruffled dense lower shrubs of fallen leaves of the dead season that also find a place to be in that forest of transcendent encounters – the very ugly and the very beautiful – again do I bring it up to remember, to remind me and you of the things that make up our being

The intimacy of love is my whistle echoing alone in the empty church before the uttered mass by the priest of my choice – and then after whirls of solitary dances finally meeting the sound of yours – the *uníssono momento* – just ready for the start of the celebrating cause

It is when I sit down, after a very hard day of work, when my mind and my body are full of tired things that need to be emptied and find reason again to start over – when I sit down and breathe with closed eyes thinking thanking God that I can indeed feel tired and then appreciate that tiredness in a moment of solitary grace – yes because if I had no work, nothing to occupy my emptiness with, I could not bear to live and would likely go mad or die of boredom and unreason for being – yes because my existence is what I make of it – just like yours and if we just sit down all the time waiting for the eternal, or Godot, he may never visit or may take over very quickly and annihilate our motive for existing, making the nothing more nothing and death an incident just like life – the incident of incidence

It is a clear day when the light penetrates the serum of our bones and brings vitamins A and D, essential nutrients to the uplifting of the soul and the fortification of the body

Or the cosy, closed-in days, with low fog dancing very near to the ground making us feel at home and sisters to the gods

It is when I say yes and yes and yes again in the game whose name I need not mention

It is when I go back home and let the smells enter my body and then travel upwards like slow arrows to the chain of my mind, that place where they rejoice in the memories that have lived there since I entered this world to suffer and to laugh

It is in the assurance that I find when I leave my home after days of forced isolation – that "Yes" that I see in the walking bodies of people that I don't even know, in the timid smile that I give to a stranger to communicate to him that I know he exists and want him to know I exist too and sometimes suffer from extreme, extreme loneliness inside my own walls – suffer and even forget that I am, trembling in fear that I may not have enough grounds to call myself a person

It is when I taste an orange and let it slide down on me imagining my own insides and how they open themselves to receive the gift of life – like lovers of love, so much love that gives kisses freely to the many passers-by swimming their liquid in and out of their entire bodies and then letting it run unbounded in the many side walks of the cities where we live and dance and cry

Or when I surprise myself in oblivion enchanted by the theories that breathe in the presence produced by the tall grass or in the brightness that passes through the closed

blinds and makes my room a church for my soul or a lake
of consoling peace – the place perfect for my being

It is when I get up and my body feels happy and restored –
ready and thankful for the commencing day – content that
the night gave me the bone marrow that I needed – content
that I am able to move – in body and mind – and that life
is there – exciting – to be lived – Abouna my Abouna – or
Isabel

It is when the lady seller of fruits – who is poor – extends
her hand offering me a ripe pear, even though she knows I
have means and need no leftovers

It is when I learn how to read stories for the first time
and my eyes become extended wheat fields – the vacant
possibilities of everything – or Isabel dancing in the open
landscape of our childhood when the church door opens
and the priest lets go

Abouna my Abouna, it is the gift

It is when I wear my orange round skirt and dance in the
wind – a moon – a sun – a star – unbounded and beautiful
like no other – ageless virgin of youth – the remembrance
of Isabel in me

Or when my blood flows out of me reminding me (and him)
of all the babies that I can still have – *uma menina dançarina*

It was so too when my grandmother, the one with blues
eyes, died, and I dressed her for the last time in that blue
dress she herself had made, knowledgeable that she was of
the days to come

Abouna my Abouna

The sonnet of red roses

The singer is a gardener too – he works between dark and light hours in the intervals that constitute the time of the moon and the time of the sun – so that he does not disturb the two celestial bodies and allows them to shine their own magnanimous splendorous tears of crystal that dance with the invisible maggots that lay on the grass

He excavates the floor in places where it is hard to impose the shovel because he tells us that the red roses, like the poetic tones of language, are best suited to grow in a floor that is composed of complicated material: of soft clay and harsh rocky morsels, of humid dark mud and dry sandy particles – it is the incidence of these, he adds, that permits him to plant the seeds very deeply into the floor of being and then have an appreciated end-result: Red-red roses

Roses so red that the light that there inhabits can compete with the already mentioned celestial bodies (the sun and the moon), and in so doing, the earth can itself become a potent fluorescent bulb with light that came from its own belly, thus owing nothing to secondary happenings

Then the gardener is a singer too – he invents light that makes the extra-terrestrial beings move around the universe in search of the holy song, the song that comes from the body of the earth, the earth with soft and harsh mud, the earth with watery and slippery dreams

They search and search in the vacuity of the air that makes the totality of what there is, and then, disconcerted with the lengthy and never ending voyage and thirsty for the red light of the red roses and the strikingly grandeur that there lays, they invent another way of moving their bodies, instantaneously becoming little green butterflies cutting the air to arrive quickly at the place where God walks and grows gowns of the sublime wine

So when you see them landing on your garden, do not be afraid, do not call the FBI, for they are merely visiting the garden that you made beautiful – the garden you planted with red-red roses, so intensely purple that music and sonnets of eternal poetry invented by men and God, can be discerned when looking deeply into their petals of blood

Do not be afraid of those strangers for they are merely visiting the garden that you made beautiful – and making you less solitary in your human small condition

I will see you in the winter

I will see you in the winter – when the rains settle in and
we slow down the walk to listen to the moments of true
when nothing makes more sense than the nothing that the
rain noise makes

I will see you then – when the water announces itself
in different moods, first slowly and sparsely then more
compact but still slow, and finally in that aggressive
thunderous manner that the gods above have of speaking
with the humans, showing either their love or their
disappointment with the deeds done during that year –
by us mere mortals who stumble to find the best ways of
encountering happiness here and there, here and there
in the intervals of unconsciousness when the logic sleeps
through us and we remember some figment of truth

I will see you in the winter – hugged by wool sweaters and
silver thick gloves so that my fingers and my breasts can
breathe in and out and the tip of my nipples can make the
exterior of what I am – and you – you will come running
to me, unmistakable lover, sure that those are the breasts
that await you and your children who still run alone in the
healthy bubbles of transparent cream that you carry in your
guarded pockets awaiting the time when being becomes
real and ceases to be an idea, a thought, a concept, a dream
of the silent night

You will come with your own sweater and your own gloves,
you too suffering from cold, yes cold but also the health and
wealth gathered throughout all the seasons of the year and

especially during the fall when the fruits of your own hard
labour finally announce themselves in abundant harvests

Come, come this winter – run to me with your vigour
underneath the sweater and grab me with gentle force,
first the outside of the sweater, where the nipples point,
as if to call you and then, with belief and still gentleness
mixed with vigour, undress me and lay me down on the
snow banks by the river Zamia – and there, under the dark
and blue skies sprinkled with yellow mimosas, make me
your procreative bride – until I scream of exhaustion and
annihilated starvation, finally having found my reason for
being – which is being and producing being – real, with
heart beats, and blood, and bones that will move by itself
and then in the circle of circular life that only knows how
to reproduce itself and generate other bones and bloods
and heart beats

I will see you in the winter
When the rains start falling, first slowly and sparsely,
then still slowly but more compact and then gradually
accelerating their rhythm inside my body so that I can have
the cool-warm bath that I have been waiting for all the
seasons of my life

Come, come – this winter
With the rain of the sky – the *lobolo* of gods
Making me the richest bride of the continent

The last supper (or the first)

The last supper – or the first worthy of the name
Cook me a meal with the crust of your dried lips
Lay my body on the open long rectangular table covered
with the cloth made of linen and silk

Sprinkle me with salt and cayenne pepper – add lemon and
parsley for the sharpness and clear freshness of the flavour
that will remind your mouth of me when I was young and
plump and full of veins with gargling blood – and then
transport that taste to my own self by way of a long kiss
that will also remind me of me when I was young and
plump and gorgeous and full of babies inside waiting to
happen

Cut the pieces of sweet bread that you made yourself with
whole grains and raisin fruits, pure and unadulterated,
collected from the fields my father worked with bare means
all his long life of a peasant of the mountains with the help
of the cows and my mother too when she was unoccupied
by other labours – and lay those on my undressed body
and then like the hungry man that you are or the candle
that does not want to dry out or the farmer that still knows
how to farm fertile land eat them piece by piece, from
bottom to top, eat them slowly until you have satisfied the
taste that you were craving which led to the preparation
of this meal – this supper which could be the last or the
first of its kind – it is really up to you – and me too – to
make it happen – to continue the ceremony of renewal and
revival lying on top of the bare table each night for the rest
of our lives – the rest which might be long – eternal even

perhaps – even though we both may think we are too old
– too old for this feast – too old for this bread – this meal
laid upon you and me on top of the bare table – all because
we still know, we still remember how to make honey – how
to produce the body and the blood of Christ and reach
the perfect union – the *chora* that the Buddha also sought
before he came to true enlightenment

The communion of the last gods – the last supper of a man
and a woman who may have thought that they were too old
for the incarnation – or the transubstantiation – but the
incantation is ancient and the ancient never dies – it revives
itself by the powers you lay upon yourself when you really
remember and descend to the cave concave and cavernous
like the twistings of wind whirls or water waves on the
placid Indian Ocean

The last supper
Or the first worthy of thee name

The making of beautiful stories

If I write down only an A then the story only exists in the possibility of what could be
If I look at the A long enough and whistle sounds of wisdom mingled with whispers of sorrows emitted by old Portuguese widows, who have long ago lost their loving men, then perhaps the story of the A will start being more than a possible idea, or the awe of waiting, to become the real harshness of those women with their black clothes hanging down their twisted legs, tired monuments full of varicose veins – caves concave

Dresses and dresses of black capes that sing long dark *fado* songs that sound like howls of lost and very needy madonnas – waiting and waiting for the day of redemption when Jesus or his Father will come down and gently deliver them from the pain of suffering by lifting them up to the azures of the skies where the air dances with you and you with it – like whirls of transcendental and pure evocations – concave caves

And if I wait even longer and do other dances and movements with that single and first letter of our long alphabet, then I will be able to find more and more stories – each letter emitting the cries of long lonely nights and the noisy murmurs of rosaries going around and around, encircling the fingers of the widows even when they lay down in bed at night and ought to enter the land of oblivion

Each letter speaking to the other like sisters of the same sorrow, nuns of the same loveless nights, desolate monastery, because widows are single, single women who must remain in the cell until the rest of their days – the old ladies of eternity who must tell their breasts and the pulse pulsating between their legs to calm, calm down, because sins will take us to the inferno flames where we will forever burn and pain

And when I arrive at the end of the line that the Z is, I know in my bones how loneliness is forged through night after night of incantations intimated by the priest – incantations told to women about what they really are and must always remain – yes because God never, never forgives – and then we die exhausted by the weight of the days that have left nothing on our scant bodies – nothing to anchor upon, except the imaginings of the perfect return

The making of sense

I can make sense of nothing if the nothing in question is
really, really nothing
But if the nothing is something that has been beaten upon
with layers and layers of meaning engendered by the courts'
judges and the careful forged constitutions, then I lose
patience and awe and start looking for other rivers where
the transparent clarity can still be seen

I can remain interested in the nothing that the light
produced by the shadow lets me see and be intrigued by the
circumflexes that mutate there in the middle of the yes and
the no
But if the neighbour turns on his harsh and fluorescent
torch in a moment of boasting needs, I then lose my way
and quickly try to find the route to the side road so that
I can recapture the nothing that I was existing in before,
where I was seeing the unseeable, that clear bareness that I
crave for and which allows me wonders out of this world –
cadences of marvellous plains full of daisies – the valleys of
my youth – when I was beautiful and bold and waited for
the stars

I can love you and you can love me as long as we, in
our loving pure ways, do not start demanding the rules
and the regulations engrained in the lines of over-
used constitutions and books of laws written by dead
conservative men who were never able to take a free swim
in the great lakes of the magnified white North

I can make sense of you and me and the idea that we are
but I cannot devise clear guidelines that would testify
to our real qualities and ways of being – all I can do is
envisage the you and the me – and then from there, I can
see the biggest sense of what we really are – free cadences
in the air of ancient Babylon amidst books and books of
nothing where the truth is written in complex symbols
of oratory speculations that can only be perceived in the
slow pronouncements of the very old priest whose eyes can
barely see

Modes of reading

I would be capable of dancing down below with ants and lionesses, the dark secret creatures of the sumptuous castles of moist moss

I would lay carefully all my limbs and let them get rotten, eternally mingling with the nothing that brings freedom and celestial marvels to my most desperate needs, the wishes and labels of a world that brings solace to my almost dead destitute self

I would light up candles and watch them wave in erotic volition to the desires of the wind that comes from afar and brings tones and secret formulas from distant continents, the twinkles of African ladies and the sorrows that their eyes carry while waiting for the true revolt to commence

I would sell my own house and all my dresses to stare at you in beatific solitude and then slide into the intimacy of your bones and your aerial body mass so that I could lose fear and find reason in the way this world works

I may pray for you when you are not aware and I may cry with open red eyes letting my water enter your river and succumb to your mesmerized way of being

I may truly hug you and let you take me until both bodies cease to feel themselves only to feel the major revelation that junction reveals

I may murmur songs to faraway little children and wait for the wave signal that informs me that they know I exist and have heard my solitary scream

I may dance and dance in the wet thick rain inside the virgin forests of incandescent millennium worlds where nothing that you value really matters and words become unwritten songs that can only be deciphered through the slow music of the ear and the low whistles of snakes

I may dream about you and descend to heaven like a cloud finally released to the tower of eternal bliss – the true, true daughter of God who has at last found the way and is never, never coming back, eternally peeking at the world but not incarnating in it, for she has completed the cycle of blood and plasma wounds and her veins will never again be inflated like her mother's and ready to burst from exhaustion

I may fall into nothing and be all that I truly desire to achieve

I may be the sole soul to enter the monastery that allows swallows to fly into secret darkness and butterflies to dance in circular motions – the house of the lord where only females are welcome because they are the preachers of sacred ancient revelations

I may be the true Buddhist who has finally found the way and is never, never coming back

The way to the river to the channel to the Main

Maydays of my youth

As a young one I would run to the empty lands of my father's land and collect the fresh leaves and the buttons of flowers and bring them to incant the walls of the houses where our sheep and cows lived, a child of May, of flowers I was, *maying* around like a spring in perpetual motion transporting the emotions that make the world have all its colours and incandescent secrets brought about by the beings of many places

I would put them there, like rosaries of merciful remembrances of times eternal that come without interruption when the month is May and the sun reaches its right scintillating position sending diagonal messages to the inhabitants down below, who are dying to be bathed in new fresh light and wake up with dew scattered on the land – clean petals of water where new days can be thought

One and the other, and the other, petals and leaves, collections collected from the bellies of the earth, which year after year, does not fail and comes to me and you praying the beauty of life and spreading the scents of the gardens of god

Petals and petals leaves and leaves of rosemary and daisies, of red and white carnations, olive marbles and laurel touches, parsley and even the smell of strong oak trees which have lived since eternity and continue to stand still when May comes and enters the inhaling modes that our noses possess

Roses and roses, petals and petals, leaves and leaves put there in circles and rows of rosaries prayed by me and heard by you creating the mass of Christ and the Resurrection of Easter when God comes again after the long and cold death of winter

I speak to the goats and the cows who are inside after spending the days on the mountains savouring these delicacies that now decorate the houses where they live, they hear me and say thank you with their breath, smoke of moist lines coming out to me and reminding me of me in them and them in me

Them, the flowers and us – the circulation of spring and the May that never, never forgets and always returns the eternal – the ring of me and you, the link of the cows and the sheep and the flowers – the pearls of the collar

I – a little girl dancing in the flowers of May getting dizzy and dizzy, dizzy like Lizzie and my seven skirts floating vapours and shades of the live season, I – a *princesa* enchanted by the enchanted, enchanting the un-enchanted, I – in the maydays of my youth

The time of cherries

The cherries came and left and I stood there in the middle
of nothing
Like an ethereal piece of trans-temporal dust collecting the
dirt of all the universes and the places beyond the last line
from where the sun rises every day to wake up your bones
and feed them with the fundamental qualities of vitamin D
– the light of pure life

I planted myself securely and steadily at the door of the
deep endless well and with my eyes in acute surveillance I
stared at the darkness that infiltrates the water immersed
in water, that translucent metaphor that glides to the centre
of the world where rats and dark butterflies live in constant
turbulence and embrace dancing amidst the ancient fire of
life

I walked slowly but with the feet profoundly grounded
on the slippery sand of the floor and aware of the stones
that can hurt my toes and pierce my veins, which as my
mother's, sometimes seem like inflated balloons ready to
burst and let blood gargle out of me

I walk in crawls like a baby-girl who suddenly knows
that the act of movement is a gift from the gods and can
enhance life's passage on this earth because one can feel
with all our body the harshness that pulsates on the crust
of the planet, that great mother that still burns viscerally in
its deep node, inside its belly – only because she loves us all
with the intensity of ravaged entrails

I chant to the trees and to the little grass and I produce incantations summoning the little rain of my youth and then allowing my body to bathe underneath so that I can become a tiny ring of pearls – or a translucent dream swimming vaguely to the entrance of the river which then becomes a sea of vast waves and colours unmemorable, which I only remember vaguely in tones that enter my body all over making it swing slightly like a tiny flower waving to the gentle breeze of May – May, the month of lilies, lilies of the valleys spread evenly like sea salt rocks celebrating life since the dawn of times when the sailors went way and the workers demanded a more communal division of the fruits of their hard labour – a labour that kills their backs and distorts the meaning of their lives

The time of cherries is full and empty like the basket of life that I can weave from the day I am born until I close my eyes and say "goodbye for now" because I might come back and be the vine that enlaces the basket that someone else will be weaving when passing through this channel and chanting this chant

Earthing my body

I hide my limbs under the earth – underneath the fourth ring of our planet, very close to the magnum opus of the stratosphere of the underground, where I sense the pure oxygen lives and I can breathe freely opening my lungs to the odour of sanctified beetles and butterflies to be

I whisper arias of forgotten melodies through the doors of my cells so that the neighbours situated below can dance and feel less alone – all because of me

I roll all my limbs with intricate sensual and certain movements to enter each sphere of the dark atmosphere where music lives and odours come to you from every corner – like blind agents whose vision is attained only through the osmosis invented by small invisible merchants of the nether lands

I whisper solitude to lost companions and they come running to me like sure galloping magnificent black horses reminding me of the beautiful sublime that true meditation and isolation can bring to oneself

Earthing my body with the mud that lies down low and below your feet and mine, very under the circles of the first ring of the stone upon which we walk every May and August, November and January, the four months of all the seasons we have

Dancing, rubbing my belly on the dark moisture, I become,
I am the black sorceress of transcontinental metaphors
travelling via the speed of scent and the intuition of light

If you

If you bring me your hollow breath, I will thank you for that with my hands completely open so that you may see all the lines of my life when I river your body with them, up and down, like the ancient Nile which tells stories of Isis and many more other divine elements

If you open the shadow underneath your molecular membrane, I will show you my scar too – the one I have underneath that point of no return when the times were unkind and my father's body came to the end of its point letting go of familiar forms and entering the bed of decomposing fall leaves – all an amalgamation of all – like Isabel's

If you tiptoe when trying to find me, I will be able to ear the sound traveling slowly but surely underneath the magnesium circle of the deeper core of the earth

If you whistle in my ear, at least once in a while, I will be able to slide to the oblivious land of the seven worlds, and in symphony with the cosmos, dance eternally in the water of my mother's womb – like silk gliding in the carrousel of childhood illusions

Capricorns of unicorns where nothing else appeals to me

I wait for you

I wait for you until my body is rotten
I wait for you until all the humidity that inhabits my cells falls down and merges with the life of the worms and the mud of the streams below
Until it bleeds its moist liquid into the five rivers that run underground, where Pluto, the Greek God, hides his evil spirits

I wait for you kneeling down for centuries and centuries like an old statue in eternal adoration
Like a broken stick putrefying itself to nourish the black slimy snakes crawling the surface of our large earth

I wait for you with a faintly lightened lantern barely calling attention to itself thinking that true love will be guided to my undying persistence without the illumination and intrusion of the great torch

I wait for you with my eyes staring at the moment when your entrance into me will restore my life into its primal and early state, that first moment when I planted myself in this position waiting, attending like a servant the expectation of my life: the arrival of the mail man or the transcendental locksmith

I wait for your with my arms open wide and circular so that I can gather the particles of you that might be guided to me, the particles that will be you when you die without finding me first so that finally we can let go and die fully

fulfilled of our encountering, entering the realm of the
underground snakes and becoming what they already are

I wait for you with my old body falling and falling into the
rotten state of nothingness
Until I smell and no one no one will dare come near me

I wait for you kneeling down like a prayer to the invisible

I wait for you like this,
Such is my undying love

I wait for you again

I wait for you in the middle of the Darfur empty desert
Under the rags that dry in the blazing sun like phantoms
waiting for the cavalcading knight who will come rushing
to bring shadow and a fresh drop of water in a tin cup

I wait with my throat breaking under the scorching sun
praying for the fresh dew of the morning to wash me down

I wait under the dancing dust in the company of children
and women cooking loving meals with wood stolen from
the empty space

I wait for you on top of the shack with my body standing
up like a flag of the nation to become

I wait for you while I scream with my lungs filled with the
dust that your robbing thugs bring in short intervals hiding
their black faces with white clothes, mounted on top of
horses with bleeding feet and neighing agonies

I wait for you washing the women who are bleeding to
death because their insides were savagely violated by your
thick phallus, I wait for you wiping their feet with white
linen cloths soaked in water from the oasis

I wait for you staring at their children's large stunned eyes
where terror and hope coincide

I wait for you like this,
Such is my love

I wait for you again and again

I wait for you on top of a moving train with my clothes
flying into freedom and the conductor waving at me with a
smile on his frank face where a thin moustache can be seen

I wait for you soaked in white milk, like the bride of the
faraway Levant where oak trees produce heavy shadows
and offer you the comfort of their thick hug, scratching
your skin like a rough but very caring lover

I wait for you licking the honeycomb without being afraid
of the cutting sting of the bees and the harsh reprehension
of the Queen Mother

I wait for you with my face stuffed under the water holding
my respiration until I can no longer remember the clarity of
my breathing lungs

I wait for you staring at the empty wall where only the
passage of the old cockroach has left her dying mark

I wait for you when I cross my legs and hold my desire in

I wait for you in the middle of the dark road holding a
bright torch and waving at the trucks racing by

I wait for you drawing butterflies in the piece of the paper
that the sand is or while the wind stops and makes your
hair stand still

I wait for you while I take a long bath and move my hands
through the channel that runs between my large breasts
with the shape of long pears trying to kiss the floor and
leave the tree that gave them life and milk all these years

I wait for you while I dress myself up for the feast
tomorrow when the church bell will toll the tolling of All
Saints Day

I wait for you in the intervals of my heart beats while my
blood decides which direction to go to give me life

I wait for you when you are not looking or when you move
seats and become distracted by your own task

I wait for you in the shadow of the handrail or the cracks of
the pot where I keep my bathing salts or the lotions for my
body

I wait for you by the grave of my grandfathers, whom I
never met, kneeling down and praying so that I can see
their memory

I wait for you in the bottle of pills I think about taking but
then decide not to, or in the sharp knife I lean meditatively
against my right pulse just above the full decided vein that
carries liquid to the many parts of my body, that great
vessel that travels thick and deep and fast to my encounter

I wait for you perched on a jacaranda naked tree in the
heights of the South African winter looking down and
seeing the flock of stunning flamingo birds, pink in their
full existence and blazing the spring skies

I wait for you in the middle of cold Lusitanian Februaries
when my father helps deliver little cows, cows that come
out all bloody and full of plasma wound

I wait for you in the middle of the night awake until
morning like a sentinel of the underground

I wait for you lying naked on the large road with arms open
and feet brought together like a Christ-ess pinned to the
Cross with blood leaving my body and entering the arteries
of the world

I wait for you like this,
Such is the persistence of my love

Craving for you

I crave the salt in your skin when I run it down with all the
crevices I possess in my unruly tongue or when I enter into
your waters through the endless liquid that inhabits your
shiny eyes, full of blackness and uncontrollable depth

I crave the liquors that you give me to drink with your glass
gently tilted into me
Or those you, in your infinite patience, offer me afterwards
when my thirst is still not annulled because I am an old
goddess with crazy long lasting appetites and pagan desires
which have been perfected time and time again through the
running of the centuries

I crave the mercury that your clock makes run when the
time that you spend with me is running out of ink, and
you, in your magic gentleness of a god of this earth, make
it atemporal – vast like the empire of the Romans, dense
like the forests of the half breasted Amazonians, slow like
the waters of Lake Elias, fast and intricately beautiful like
the stunning springbok of the Great Karoo of South Africa
that flies in mid air because she is a pro in the execution of
somersaults – perhaps running from hunters, human and
animal, who in their envy of the truly beautiful want to
annihilate the divine dance

I crave the minute sounds that we in our silence are capable
of producing and then the time that comes after that – an
ethereal being of magic mantras that the priest of that
religion has taught us how to pray in perfect rhythm – with
drums and violins and thin flutes and then loud guitars

and expanded thick raucous saxophones – the blues of the eternal slaves of this world – of the Blacks and the Egyptians and the Persians and the Athenians and the Spartans of low caste even though some of these are often thought to be the fathers of democracy, but in reality one must remember that they forgot to mention the slaves in their perfect Republic or properly name the misnamed Barbarians – the Republic of theoretical equality and freedom, or the blind review of justice, like the medication that the doctor gives you that is not really a medication but you think it is because you are told it is and so you really become better – the placebo is the proper name, the name given by the doctors, the Republic of theoretical equality and freedom, or the blind review of justice, only that

I crave for you in the movement of the ceiling shadows, those events that happen when we are intertwined in the work that is most important to us and which we do ritualistically every season of the day or night or early morning, just before the noisy and excited chatter that the birds, who perpetually live in a summer country, start making – uncontrollable in the deadly energy of their overly present life

I crave for you when I fall down and have no one, no one to kiss my booboo
When I chant to the wind in beautiful forgiveness of my self and you are not there to witness the astounding quality of my performance
When I cry out of love for thee and you are not there to wipe my tears with the humid saliva of your entire body

I crave, for you, now and then, now and then
But sometimes I stop craving
Because I find in myself the true idea of what you are and how you are

Call it the supra-vision of the thinking philosopher
Or the divine vision of a simple human
Who, in her aloneness of living, uses the imagination to survive the harshness of this life

Isabel,
In the death of my body

I am not alive today
And I feel this feeling often
Ever since the times of my being
And the remembrance of being
As if death (and all it entails) has always lived in me
Preventing me from ever or very rarely feeling life in its luscious fullness
As if in the infinite doom of times I am the primal source of pain and decay

I feel that my body is going into the death realm
As if I am joining my beautiful friend Isabel
Who left just a month ago in the fall of that sullen November
She was young and sage and she left me and everyone else
Premature announcement of what is to come when my body and yours go
Down under and melt with the rest forming the *chora* of death
Which will become life and death and life and death again
A circle of circular and macabre incantations that cannot be stopped

This body of mine feels heavy like a thousand iron bars
Where nothing, nothing can feel the light of flight
Incantatory spoiled butterflies mourning the future
Drained by the power of life and death
And the memory of Isabel
The *saudade* of you, my beloved, singing into my every day

My darling Isabel

The death of my body precedes the death of your soul
Your soul feels the profound sadness of the memory of the body
Which no longer is
The cells that break down little by little and then cease to be
Taking with them the memory of my soul (and yours)
When I (and you) walked outside in springs of life
The scents of rosemary and laurel and inebriating carnations, red and white
And those with pinkish stripes too, found up there in the mountains of Adsamo
Or transcendence
Engulfing the pheromones of our entire skin blanket
With the soft latent winds of the upper skies (clean and sensual)
Waving our womanly forms and kissing the kissable
I am taken by the solstice of life
The solstice of winter
As my body shuts down, to meet Isabel's, my beloved friend
Who left just a month ago in the sullen sudden fall of November
A last tear invading my self, which still reclaims and claims life, her life, my life

Today I feel the heaviness of a thousand bars
A thousand deaths upon my back
As if I have lived countless times and died many deaths
Or eaten endless Christmas presents
Intoxicating my body and killing it and others before the time

Isabel my love
I feel you in my body

Its tremulous life at the verge of complete annihilation
It's painful
Visceral
And so existential
Like giving birth to your monthly blood
Isabel my love
Where are you
In me
Or I in you

In the death of my body

My body becoming

My body comes to me in waves of melons and peaches
When the morning dew falls slowly into my bellybutton
The honeycomb of the start sweetening me up like the primal sheet of the universe

I wake up from my solitude and embrace the abode that I am
The hymn of the hymen, the hymen of the soul, the solace encountered after years and years of eternal, long, profound and hurting loss

A mass of hexagonal wax, a mass of cells built by bees
All the bees yellow and white and black
With sharp antennas, fully aware of the eternal work ahead of them
Building the quilt where finally I will lie down
Like the *rainha* of the *rainhas*

My body becoming
My body is

Coming upon you

I came upon you one night
Breeding bread flowers for my soul
Open my legs wide and silently
And I will sink into you
The sweet of god and I bathe my solitude
One hundred years of it
Like the magical and the realist
In the chrysanthemums, the flowers of death, and life too
Engulfing my thin body
And bringing me the sun that I shiver for
Full of moment
Fill me with flowers and bread and soul
Rose me smell me with all the plants you have in you
Vaster and grander
Sing me a song
That will be the prayer of my nether nights, nether delights
And burning days
When extreme cold and unbearable heat nullify the eternal
hymn
This cell of mine
Fill it will roses and roses, flowers of all kinds
Lay upon it
Like the sanctuary that it is
Like you never did with anyone else
Then make greedy love, greedy for the profoundness of the
uncanny
With scenes and scenes to become
Under the antidote that will emerge from your consecrated
words
The ugly becoming so beautiful

Bleeding for the being

I sit at the veranda
When my karmic model informs me
Of my existential reflection

I play skip in the shades
Thinking of my empty spheres filling the world
And dreaming about how to enter the stars
And hang out with the pollen
That flies invisible above the earth's magnanimous crust
In each season of the year
Even in winters gelid
And falls almost dead
Manoeuvres of my own
To break the silence of my hurt being
The beat of the hymen of my significance

I play solitude scenes just before the sun goes down under
I stop for a moment to gaze at the blazing blast that is the purple fire of the firing sky, bleeding and bleeding not to end, jealous of the other world that will receive light and afraid of the dawn to come

I play skip
And I play solitude
By the veranda of my deciphering days
Trying to become myself

I open the palm of my hand
For all the stars to find place in it
One by one

One by one
I see the blazing of the Gemini sisters
And Andromeda, the northern constellation located directly
south of Cassiopeia, between Pegasus and Perseus
And even the red burned power of the faraway Pluto
And the stunning light of its biggest moon, Charon

All of them in the very centre of my palm
And then I become imploded with power
And explode into nothingness
A cosmic revelation
A titanic abracadabra

My body comes

My body comes to me in half peaches and full melons
Like life dripping in and out of me
The moon in half crescent rising to the full cry of the wolf

My body comes to me in half peaches and full melons
Like fresh, fresh dew
Of the morning to be
The days to become

I lay alone in the middle of the road
To receive it
And howl to the bright silver matron
Who brings me to the fullest of my season

Coming from deep

Long time ago I would imagine the movement of his body
When the days would be silent and the cells would be
singing slow cadences of almost dying stars

My father is an old man now, a sturdy villager who never
believed that it is the earth that moves and the sun that
stays in the same place when the seasons come and go

He was much sturdier when he was young and the days
came and went, came and went, like the many Junes that he
passed through eviscerating the earth to feed all the boys
and girls he gave to when my mother opened the fertile land
that she had in the endless garden living inside her belly

He was brusque and sure that the season would give fruits
to the needy and that life, the only thing that this world can
be, is a line straight and deep, the depth that leads you to
the centre of the earth's cycle and allows you to see all there
is to see

Now he is not well, I am far away and I listen to his
sporadic gasps for life when he says he will get out of bed
the next morning, he will and he will go see the cows that
he helped raise and taught how to plough the land

He stays in days and days, nights and nights, closed to the
hours that run outside in the seasons that slow his body
more and more

His limbs and his cells are affected, defected by the passage of time and the making of many boys and girls who called him father for nearly a century

I am far away from his dying body, and in this moment of death and solemn silence of the cells, I want to hug his evading body and his mind, that mind that has suffered the AVC of cardiovascular disease and the colossal vagueness of a liquid that does not run like before when love and life swam inside him and my mother, vigorous candours of pressing life

My father is dying, and I am very far away from the slow life that still runs in him
Coming from deep, very deep, the depths of time and memory
Of glories and springs of perpetual maying days
When everything was

I look for you

I look for you in the cuts that I make on my fingers when I cook small meals for myself at night and then I look for you again in the blood running and mixing with the green leaves that I ingest slowly, the body of Christ, in its full bloody and suffering form, like a sacrilege cannibal

I look for you in the blood and plasma that I give birth to every twenty-eight days so regular is the life that is trying to find a beat inside me

I look for you in those dead morsels of tissue mixed with all the vitamins that I ate that month, I mix them in my hand as if killing them again, perhaps to feel responsible for a crime that is truly yours, not mine, I mix them and then I eat them hoping that death will be redeemed into life

I look for you in the sweat that my body leaves on my bed sheets, I keep those sheets unwashed for months and months so that my chances of finding you become greater and greater

I look for you when I close my eyes and enter the bright shadows of the wonder under world, that precinct where Pluto, the Greek God, keeps guard of good and evil

I look for you in the space that separates each of my five fingers or in the hollowness of my bellybutton

I look for you in the slow dance of the curtains of the living room when it's very hot outside and time seems to have stopped in a moment of goodness

I look for you in the shadows of the white lilies and in the discrete fluorescence of the hydrangeas, both growing vividly in the savage mountains of the land where I was born

I look for you in the waters of the river Zamia that run with the placidity of a tired but sure love affair

I look for you in the spots I can see on the surface of the moon when it's fully illuminating our planet, and I do so lying down in concentration with my back on the wet grass, allowing the dew to cover my entire body and making it the river of drops and drops, one by one, one by one

I look for you in the antennas of the butterflies and in the black and yellow rings of the busy honey bees, and then I also search the fogs of the winter and the thunder of the summer to find pieces of you that might be scattered through the various rings that constitute the universe

I look for you in the empty nests of the startled birds and wait for the beginning of birth to arrive

I look for you in the many tiny spaces that exist between all the hairs I have on my head, slowly putting my fingers through each and each, each and each

I look for you in the wideness of the landscape when only silence fills the golden chant of nothingness

I look for you at dawn – in that moment between the yes and the no when everything becomes a possible theory

I look for you in the middle of the undulating wheat fields
when their colour is between green and eternal golden
beige

I look for you in the bareness of the black board before I
inscribe the words in and sully the neatness that could have
been you

I look for you in the noise that my feet make when I
walk on stony roads or in the silence that comes when I
choose somersaults and avoid the chatter of the rough and
irregular ground

I look for you when I sleep with my eyes open in the
middle of the day and the rhythm takes me into the
concaves of caves sliding me into the beautiful oblivion

I look for you when I stare at the waters of Lake Elias and
see the sheen that my face is capable of producing under
your translucent guided brilliance

I look for you on the broken seashells that pierce my naked
walking soles making my blood soak in the sand – that vast
sheet of immense softness, the nothingness of my ethereal
mimes

I look for you in the remembrance of my infancy when I
used to put my head on my mother's lap – when she would
rummage my hair with her thick deformed fingers and I
would smell the many cooked meals and plasma wounds of
all the births she gave to

I look for you in the pure unadulterated taste of the
avocado – that fruit full of healthy oils and then in the salt

that I add to it, and then again in the taste of both melting in my mouth and making me strong and able

I look for you in the taste of the green apple when I first sink my beautiful white teeth into it – those teeth that kept their lasting health despite the fact that I used to be a hard-core bulimic, constantly throwing my body into the toilet bowl, and wasting it into the putrefying gutter of the dirty underground where evil spirits can cause havoc when Pluto, in a moment of optimistic sentiment, is not keeping a careful watch and decides to search for the little flowers that might grow even there, in his main headquarters, where the sun very seldom finds it in him to forgive and peek in to wave a gentle hello

I look for you in your shiny manly shoes and then in your careful tied tie – and then not satisfied with what I see there, I look for you in your naked vulnerable image which I imagine only to satisfy my most profound yearning – the yearning of a woman who cannot stand the pretension of exacerbated and insecure masculinities

I look for you in the smell that I gather when I put my hand in that forbidden place that I keep firmly locked in with the pressure of my crossed legs

I look for you when I shave my hair and pass my hand through the crisp, clear, clean crust of my eternal skull where the memory of all my African ancestors pulsates with the vigour of an incandescent fountain of life

I look for you in the letters of the Greek alphabet between the Alpha and the Omega and in that vacant space I meditate about your way of being – and at points become almost satisfied with my theories about what it is that you

might be, what it is that pulsates in your carnal bloody
body full of visceral organs

I look for you when, in the deep desperation and bareness
of the moment, I imagine the many complete instants
I have had in the pasts of my life – and this, this is an
exercise that I do often so that the actual emptiness of the
moment will be filled with some reason of being, a reason
for being and at least the re-imagining of happiness

I look for you at Sunday service when the minister of God
reads from the Old Testament – that part of the Book
about the Hebrews and their dream about finding their
promised land, or the other part from the testament when
the shepherd of mere sheep becomes the actual pastor of
God by the great force of some metaphoric metamorphic
trans-mutative consubstantiation, transubstantiation – the
intervention that testifies to the true truth of truth

I look for you in the inflated varicose veins my mother
has all over her deformed legs and then in that nervous
moment when I wait for them to burst

I look for you in my niece's plump little legs which I kiss
with the laughing eagerness of a stunned child who has
discovered the perfect degree of composure in the tissue of
her own DNA – and then again, when I stare at her long
dark lashes and the even darker eyes peeking underneath

I look for you in that map that I keep close to my hand – in
the rivers and vessels of rivers, the ridges, creases and slopes
of mountains and hills, in the fauna and flora of the five
continents, in the seas and oceans, in the lakes and puddles
of fresh and putrid smelly water, in the rotten fishes and
the dead carcasses of the massive elephants of the Karoo

hunt down by ivory fanatics, in the papayas that I pick up
from the floor of Brazil

I look for you in the dense intricate forests, minutely
searching for the tip of your finger under the dead pine
needles and I rummage the thick moist moss quilts looking
for the needle in the haystack, the needle that will bite me
and make me bleed, bleed of life and happiness

I look for you in the milk that I make my breasts produce
when I have doubts about my reproductive capacities and
motherly instincts, I squeeze them with force and they hurt
and hurt and sometimes I see blood in lieu of milk leaving
them and crying my life out of me

I look for you when I feed grain to the chicken and when
they run after me looking for more

I look for you like this,
Such is the patience of my love

I am a novel,
A novel of my own making

Reading is a difficult exercise. Read me horizontally and then vertically and then stop and look at the spaces between the words that I inscribe here in this place, where before there was nothing except the idea of me, my memory vacant in the liquid of the whiteness that tries to escape a destiny.

Reading is a difficult exercise. Read me again and again and again. Go back to the other documents that I may have inscribed in some white paper where there was nothing before my ink came upon it, to inflict upon the page and dirty its sheen pristineness, like the love that my grandmother made, the one with blue eyes, and also the one with black, pitch black eyes, the madonnas of her times, fooled by the illusion of the lord's words.

Read me without the knowledge of me but read in me the knowledge that I may have given you before, here and there, there and here. In the pulse of nothing, in the sigh of sadness, in the lamp lighten, low and persistent, when my mother who never never prays gets up scared and starts invoking incantations to the saint like an extreme devout, the saint São Gregório, please do not send thunder, please *senhor*, please my darling saint, do not send light and punishment, crime and punishment to this slave. What I am is everywhere. It is here and there, there and here.

When you wake up at night lost in the dream you could not have, get up slowly and firmly and walk around your house: each compartment, each corner where the dust might be hiding, despite the fact that you are a cleaning maniac and spend nights and days erasing the dirt that is your life and my life. Go up and down the stairs several times, like a *romaria* of the lord and feel the wood of the handrail thick and rough in your hands, let it slide, do not let it stop you because you think it will make your hands unfeminine, unappealing, cracked with cracks. Go on and on through each corner of the house, the mug, the plate, the sink, the mat, the mad cat who dreams about eating the bread, the body of Christ given in church by padre Amaro and stolen by the drunk Dionisia. Go to the bed again where you could not dream. Touch the quilt first and then slip your fingers slowly through each layer that you have put there, one upon the other to keep the winter off, feel one and the other, one by one by one until you can dream the sweat you have left there over the years, when you thought you were too cold and did not dare to take off one of the layers laying there upon you, making you the monument that you are today: tall and rough, uncertain and confused, greedy sometimes and gentle, so gentle that it makes me cry ...

Go in circles, circular until you feel dizzy, dizzy like Lizzie, whom I remember being kind when I was new at the job of selling, selling memberships to the top people, people looking for the form they already had but forgot how to reach. Then, when all is profoundly checked, leave the house, the dust, the curtains, the position of the chair, the keys eternally on top of that strange table as if waiting for the letter with the big news to open the secret door, a door that will lead to the cave, concave, full of wells and wind mills, and glass palaces where the monster of Montesinos in the dark scares you to death, Sancho Pança and his lord, crazy *cavaleiros, donquiteiros,* travelling to the nether nether spheres. When all of that is checked, all of that and more, leave the neighbourhood, do not close the door because you might need to peek in to remember the position of the forgotten.

Walk naked through the sidewalks carefully cared for and crafted, leave them and enter the tortuous terrains exploding outside of the neat direction of your feet, enter the mud that eats you in like the little *colombiana* of whom Isabel Allende speaks, I also speak of her in the story I wrote in the other language, the other language that I also write to become more concave and full of hollow.

Then slide to the greens and the dries of the savannah, jump to the insular Greek Islands in one single vast movement and speak to the poets who are also highly skilled shoemakers, swim to the bottom of life, become transcontinental, transparent, translucent ...

Become transcontinental, transparent, translucent ...
Reading and writing
Writing and reading

I am a novel
A novel of my own making
A ball of white cotton thread that guides you to pieces and particles of me
The limbs, the cells, the blood, joined, joining the river, the lake Elias, the sea

I am a novel
Of my own making

The imperfect perfect unravelling of the spirit

Or the memory of being

About the Author

Irene Marques holds a PhD in Comparative Literature, a Masters in French Literature, a Masters in Comparative Literature and a Bachelor of Social Work. She is a bilingual writer (English and Portuguese), has taught African and Caribbean literatures, comparative and world literature, literary theory, writing and rhetoric and Portuguese at the Ontario College of Art and Design University and the University of Toronto for over 10 years. She has also worked at the Centre for Addiction and Mental Health for 14 years. In 2007 she spent a year in South Africa on a Mellon postdoctoral fellowship conducting research related to early colonial encounters between African women and male European colonialists. Her academic publications include the edited volume *The Works of Chin Ce: A Critical Overview* (2007), the manuscript *Transnational Discourses on Class, Gender, and Cultural Identity* (2012) and numerous articles in international journals including *African Identities: Journal of Economics, Culture and Society, Research in African Literatures,* and *CLCWeb: Comparative Literature and Culture.* She is the author of a short story collection, *Habitando na Metáfora do Tempo: Crónicas Desejadas (Dwelling in the Metaphor of Time: Desired Chronicles)*, as well as the poetry collections, *Wearing Glasses of Water* and *The Perfect Unravelling of the Spirit.* She emigrated to Canada from Portugal at the age of 20.

About Her Work

What impresses most in Irene Marques' first book of poetry, *Wearing Glasses of Water*, are the expansive situations she creates. Rarely does small abide over large, or unadorned show instead of ornate, for this Portuguese-born Canadian writer revels in abundance and lush colourings. Call this fat poetry, not thin. At its best it reminds me of the magic realism of Gabriel Garcia Marquez: everything writ large and interconnected. Marques continually welcomes us into her world with poetic leis and figurative dances. We come to recognize her through over-exposure, exaggeration, generous sloppiness, and glee. The poems knit together with repeated images and words so that the whole assumes a universal feel. When she writes straight out smartly we're caught unaware ... Marques has a clear ability to turn a poem and make it her own.

– *Arc: Canada's National Poetry Magazine*

[T]he essence of Marques' poetry is a peep into the complex dimensions and psychological states of being, of creativeness and inventiveness with the Word, of themes and motifs of libidinal drives or instincts, of internal emotional conflicts where individual impulses and needs must be placed in ethical resolution with social or moral obligations. [With] Irene Marques and *Wearing Glasses of Water*, the world is consequently geared for renewal, the universe set to expand in its revolving and perpetuating order – an order that needs must leave behind for all humanity a glow of transformation. Thenceforth we can strive in wearing our teardrops, ("glasses of water") knowing that life deals these experiences to us in an effort to imbue meaning and purpose to terrestrial existence, which also means – as some of our own poets would hint – our filling the higher ethics to the craft and aesthetes of our various creative callings.

– *African Journal of New Poetry*

Literature can certainly have a sex and it always has a gender, even if in the case of *Habitando na metáfora do tempo*, the gender is indeterminate. Textuality is revealed through the eroticism of language, a language that can be seen under the angle of poetry, or poetic chronicle, or philosophical poetry, or even as poetic-prosaic philosophising, bringing doubt to the textual matrix. Literature then becomes equivalent to the "primal orgasm"...where we detect the "Fall of the Angel" due to sin: the pressed down Catholicism returning eternally in this writing, a writing unable to liberate itself from it, creating a space for a symbolic Salome, the dancer and fatal woman, who appears in this book.

– Professor Pires Laranjeira, Universidade de Coimbra, Portugal

The Perfect Unravelling of the Spirit ties the secular rituals of everyday to sacred rites of passage, binding language to love and longing, and to the livelihoods that are Irene Marques' birthright. These poems bring new and old worlds into dialogue, and poetry into the presence of timeless, generous spirits.

– Edward Chamberlin, *If This is Your Land, Where Are Your Stories?*

MIX
Paper from responsible sources
FSC® C100212

Printed in June 2013
by Gauvin Press,
Gatineau, Québec